NA

G000164453

by Joanne St.Clair

Naked Raver (First edition 2012)

© Joanne St.Clair, 2012

All rights reserved.

Illustrations by Daniel Orlick © 2012

ISBN: 9781468049008

Designed by Joanne St.Clair

Printed by Create Space.

For all you Naked Ravers

…….the world over.

as truththe naked few nudities There so are objectionable

There are few
nudities so
objectionable
as the naked
truth

Agnes Repplier

I NEVER thought that in my lifetime I would become a messenger for the Universal Laws of Truth. As youths we are conditioned to believe that leadership roles of this nature are reserved for those ordained by a great committee, as though the sacred torch can only be passed down through a known and defined lineage as documented in the history books and sanctioned by those in robes.

And yet, the same divine hand that blessed the spiritual leaders of the past has, for some reason, pointed her finger at me, instructing me to go forth and share the Universal Laws of Truth that lift humanity from the jaws of illusionary power, birth-right hierarchies, and man-made spiritual legislations - systems and procedures that exist to benefit a few whilst perverting the hopes and dreams of many.

This divine presence revealed her beauty and majesty to me whilst I was confined in a police cell. Stripped naked, my only companion was the Truth within me, and what I experienced that day changed my whole perception of life. In the space of just a few hours, I witnessed first hand the result of what happens when humanity drops its ego charade; and of the global effect when genuine happiness abounds for everyone, every where. This experience was so profound that my entire life was flipped upside down, resulting in me closing the door on an existence I had spent my whole life creating.

Turning my back on my career, my home, my family and friends, and everything else that was associated with 'me', I embarked on a journey, my only desire being to fully understand the practical application of the Universal Laws of Truth and what it means for an individual when they commit to consciously live by these Laws.

What you are about to read is a true story. Some names have been changed and several conversations have been placed within fewer settings for ease of conveying the information, but on the whole this story is told exactly as it happened.

Many times I have wondered what it would be like to stumble upon this fascinating story for the first time as a reader, because it is as much a sacred parable for living as it is the true story of an individual who demanded to see beyond the commonly worn veil of existence.

Enjoy, learn and share, but more than this, just dare to believe in the possibility of it all.

Joanne

The blind receive

sight blind receive their The their sight

walk And lame

And the lame walk

the

MY FRIEND is called Sarah. She is labelled by society as disabled. Her bones break easily and have done ever since she was a child. Because of this affliction, one of her hip joints gives the appearance of being permanently dislocated as it struggles to carry the mass of her body. And metal pins and other gadgets serve the function of support structures in her legs, her main bones having either crumbled away or snapped in several places at some point during her twenty-four year life.

Sarah is also over-weight by around fifty pounds, a problem that is a constant source of frustration to her and one she readily blames on her brittle bone disease (and not on her addiction to carbonated drinks and chocolate). The combination of these physical side effects means that she has severe mobility issues, being able to walk only short distances (unaided), with the need of a wheelchair (along with someone to push it) for when the going gets tough.

This is her first time in Amsterdam, a city she has always longed to come to but has never had anyone to come with. It is a destination I have enjoyed on several occasions, and so I decided to organise a short trip and accompany her, to show her the sights of the city as well as some of my favourite places to hang out.

SARAH and I are in our hotel room sitting on a corner of one of the beds, both looking down at an opened box of Philosopher's Truffles, the strangest looking magic mushroom species I have ever seen. I say to her, in the affirmative, "I will eat the whole box."

"How many are you *meant* to take?" she asks, slightly nervous, this being the first time that she has ever come face-to-face with such a product.

"I haven't got a clue," I reply. "I'll just do them all."

I had first set my eyes on the Philosopher's Truffle two years ago, but intuition told me that I wasn't ready for them. They reminded me of the rotten teeth of a monster – huge, ugly, irregular shaped solid balls - filled to the brim with nature's finest (and strongest) hallucinogenic trip, the journey of which I wasn't prepared to embark on.

When I saw them in a glass cabinet in one of Amsterdam's Smart shops, I was mesmerized at the sheer intensity they conveyed to me back then, as though these Truffles carried an unspoken warning for me and me alone, which said: *These are the point of no return.*

I wasn't ready to submit myself to them at the time, to climb into *their* boxing ring and test my staying power, because I knew that I didn't have it in me (mentally) to come out on top. But today I AM ready. I believe that I do have it in me.

I feel it.

I know it.

And I intend to dive right in at the deep end, even though I don't know how deep this end actually is.

Sarah asks, "What will happen?"

I tell her, "I do not know. I have never taken them before."

"What should *I* do?" she questions, "because you know I'm not having any."

"Just be there until the end," I reply. "This is all I ask of you. Whatever happens, just stay with me. Ok?"

One by one I consume the contents of the box, masticating slowly to ensure that every bit is savoured, like a child secretly eating a selection of the most prized and yet forbidden chocolates.

Whilst waiting for my body to process the Truffles, I notice Sarah staring at me, watching me like a cat eyes a mouse and anticipating my every move.

"Come, let's go!" I order, the effects starting to seep into my consciousness.

We leave the hotel, heading into the heart of the city. The wheelchair offers Sarah some support as she pushes it through the narrow cobbled streets. Linking her arm, I notice that she is walking slowly until I start to get animated and excited, and then I see her break out into a faster walk as though she is excited too. So together we speed up, talking and giggling like school children doing something that we know we shouldn't be doing even though it feels good.

We enter a busy market square where an open-air art exhibition seductively calls to passing patrons. Walking immediately in front of us is a man who, in his desire to see the paintings on display, strains his neck to look whilst keeping himself at a notable distance (most people would simply move closer). Because of the awkward position of his head, he doesn't see a kerb in front of his feet, resulting in him tripping over it and almost falling flat on his face.

The whole scenario makes me laugh. Not a quiet laugh, but a loud, hearty, genuine laugh, causing some people to turn and look.

After the man regains his composure he becomes very annoyed at my laughter, shouting *It is not that funny!* but his voice sounds more like the bark of a large dog than it does a human shout. And the way his mouth moves also resembles that of a canine.

Unable to contain myself, I laugh even more and, as I do, Sarah's excitement grows. She too is laughing, and is moving faster than I have ever seen her move before, as if the jovial and upbeat pace of the moment is fuelling her bones, causing her feet to glide over the terrain with ease. She is oblivious to this fact though, unaware of how nimble she suddenly appears on her legs. Usually a walk that lasts more than five minutes drains her energy, leaving her short of breath and in need of some respite.

"This is Amsterdam," I announce with the mannerism of a circus ringmaster, officially welcoming Sarah to the city, "home of hedonism and coffee shops. If you can get away with anything in life.......it is in Amsterdam.

Want to smoke yourself into a stupor, in public?..... It can be done..... in Amsterdam.

Red lights, shop windows, girls and women of all shapes, sizes and price.

Drug dealers in alleyways,
Loud bars, crazy people,
Sunshine, laughter,
Me,you,.....
And a wheelchair!"

WE ARE in a coffee shop/bar sat by the window. Sarah sits with her back to the wall and I with my back to the public. The effects of the Philosophers Truffles are in full swing now, and I am seeing Sarah in a *new way*.

It is as if she has temporarily lifted a *veil* from her face - a subtle layer that cannot normally be seen with the naked eye - and underneath this veil is a person I have never known nor have ever seen before.

As I look more intently, I realise that the veil I am seeing is Sarah's *ego*, a *deliberately fashioned* outer layer that she has gotten used to hiding behind, as though there is a *real* Sarah that shies away just so this ego can masquerade itself in public. I see her ego so vividly that it is like looking at a set of clothes that have developed a personality of their own.

I clearly notice that Sarah's ego parades itself in a pity-me dress, somewhat dowdy and restrictive; and shoes that are worn down on the heels, heavily trodden along the road of *no one understands*. It is well-worn attire, tatty and old fashioned in areas, which seems completely ill fitting now.

Sarah is capable of much more than she has previously shown me. I saw how she virtually ran over the cobbled streets earlier. As she sits before me, I struggle to even believe in her disability anymore, because it appears to be nothing more than a role that she has *adopted*.

And so I tell her, straight, my words causing a change of expression on her face.

After a pause for thought, during which time I observe Sarah as closely as she had watched me in the hotel room, she tells me that she is shocked by my revelation: first of all for saying that I don't buy into society's *disadvantaged* label, and secondly for telling her that she is *beautiful*.

"You're the first person to ever tell me that I am beautiful," she says. "What makes you say this?"

I reply, "There is a different *you* inside, as though your skin is just keeping warm a stunning person who is never seen by the world. Sarah, I see it! As I speak to you I don't even recognise your face. It's as if I am looking into the very depths of your soul at a totally different woman, and she is genuinely beautiful!

It's you, but the face is different, perfect even. Her smile is warm, whilst her eyes convey a depth of compassion and sincerity that jumps right out at me, like a 3D effect movie, as though I could physically reach out and touch her face with my hand. Right now she is smiling at me, and she is glowing. I don't know who she is Sarah, but she is in there, *inside you*, and she is making her presence known to me."

As we are talking, I feel the effects of the Philosophers Truffles intensify, sharpening my powers of perception whilst totally relaxing my mind and body. Waves of energy bounce off my skin, giving me a sensation of lightness from head to toe.

I hear a group of rowdy men behind me, and an upbeat song plays on the jukebox. A tingle works its way through my body as though my nerves are being massaged by a gentle electrical shock. It feels so nice that I jump up from my seat and turn around, shouting *Yeeaaahh* in excitement.

Everyone in the bar looks at me, and so I smile - a knowing, mischievous grin signalling that *the party has arrived*. The place goes quiet, so I shout *Yeeaahhh* again, this time putting my hands in the air.

The table of rowdy men break the moment's silence with a loud cheer of appreciation, so I call out to them, "Who wants a hug?"

The majority of them reply, eagerly, with either a *yes* or *I do*. I don't imagine it is a difficult decision for them to make: I am a curvy size ten with a natural 34E bust. This may be the closest some of them have ever come to such a svelte figure, and no doubt they want to make the most of what I am offering.

Feeling happy and elated, I lean over the table where they are sitting and hug several of them, after which I encourage them all to do the Mexican wave.

As we are laughing, the doorman taps me on the shoulder and tells me to go and sit down. At first I don't hear his words because the music is loud, so he repeats what he has just said, pointing towards Sarah and the table by the window. Thinking that he is joking, I start laughing and, in a more serious tone, he threatens to evict me from the venue.

Clearly surprised but still with a smile on my face, I ask, "What, you are going to evict me, my friend over there and that portable commode that's propped up against the window?"

He nods his head.

"This is Amsterdam," I giggle, "what threat are we?"

When he sees that I am not taking him seriously, he starts to get flustered and orders me to leave. Immediately! At first I don't move, innocently assuming that he is having a laugh.

My response makes him mad and he threatens to call the police.

"Calm down," I say in a jovial manner. "If it means that much to you, I will leave." As I speak to him I look directly into his eyes, expecting to see the sign that he is joking. But I don't. Instead I see *his* veil, like the one I saw on Sarah, and then I see *beyond* it, recognising a different person hibernating inside of him too, a person who is gentle, welcoming, and who doesn't stress over such trivial details.

When I see this I know that I cannot take his frustration seriously because it is false. Totally false! This doorman is doing nothing more than playing a role - a contrived character on life's stage - but to the extent that he has forgotten he is merely an actor and genuinely believes he is the leading role that he has assigned himself.

To double-check his disposition, I ask him again if he is serious, reminding him that I am only laughing and that it really is nothing to get worked up about. I explain that my friend and I are the least threatening people in here.

He tells me (still with an angry tone and now with a red tinge to his face) that we are not the sort of clientele he wants in the bar and that we are to leave. Now!

When I hear his response I cannot contain my laughter anymore. I motion, as best I can, for Sarah to get our coats whilst I collect the wheelchair. I continue laughing as I clumsily manoeuvre through the narrow doors, cheered on by the table of rowdy men, with some of them even applauding to show their support. Finding the situation I have been presented with as being hilarious, I struggle to contain myself anymore, the effect of which is loud, hearty, genuine laughter.

When we get outside, Sarah flings her body into the wheelchair. She is tired and in need of some respite. I tell her I will push but I cannot stop laughing, the handles of her chair offering me vital support and preventing me from simply lying down and laughing my head off.

I have seen mass brawls, catfights, drunken punch-ups, illegal drug dealing, and many other tense interactions in which people have been ordered to leave a venue. But a female who is peace-fully elated during the day, in the middle of a city reputed for its tourist trade in drugs, prostitution, sex shops, peep shows, and whatever else goes on undercover of darkness?

There's a first for everything in life, and this is surely one of those occasions. If I wasn't the main character of the moment then I may never believe in its sheer lunacy.

These thoughts make me laugh even more until it feels as though my mouth is about to spread its wings and fly away. At this climax with my laughter, I get a strong feeling that the happiness coming out of me needs another way of expressing itself, and so I naturally start to sing. The words *'I am so happy! I am so, so happy'* play out a melody of their own making, aided by a beat brought forth from many wonderful memories.

We are in another one of Amsterdam's busy cosmopolitan market squares, where bars and cafes with outside tables are positioned around a large, open paved area. Unsure of where to go, and not really wanting to go anywhere, I carry on singing – at people in the cafés and at passers-by - looked upon complacently by Sarah.

As an elderly man walks past I hold out my arms to him. He comes towards me with his outstretched hands and we dance, both smiling and fully appreciative of the joy we are sharing. Our dance is brief but my singing continues.

And then, from seemingly out of nowhere, like a wild cat creeping up on its unsuspecting prey, a riot van arrives and stops a short distance away, causing me to momentarily pause and look towards it. In total disbelief I observe a group of police officers (with weapons) alight from the van and walk towards Sarah and I.

With an agenda of law enforcement, one which seeks to protect the citizens of Amsterdam with dignity, honour and respect, the police officers encroach upon us, most with serious looks on their faces but a couple of them with the questioning look of *why are we all needed here?*

As they form a semi-circle around us, a stand off that would be more suited to the capture of an international fugitive, I glance at Sarah, the whole scene causing a stunned expression to etch itself on her face.

I can honestly say that in all of my life, I have never witnessed anything more comical or more absurd than what is unfolding in front of me, and as the farcical reality of the moment sinks in, my whole insides erupt into a form of laughter that even I didn't know existed. It is the sort of uncontrollable laughter that grips a baby when it discovers something very, very funny, and the more I close and open my eyes to confirm that this is really happening, the greater the hysterics of the moment hit me.

The only thing that I can possibly do in this situation to channel the feeling within is to laugh even more, and so I laugh so loud, so heartily, and so genuinely that tears unceasingly roll down my face until, like before, the laughing gives way to the happiest song I have ever heard.

"What is wrong with you?" a bewildered policeman asks as he handcuffs me and moves me towards the van.

For a brief moment my entire life flashes through my mind and I become possessed by an uplifting voice that knows no limits to its vocal range. I do not feel the need to speak because the song is doing it for me, like a humming bird whose music is part of its every movement.

The policeman ushers me inside the van, putting me into a seat next to a window. Treated like a high security prisoner, I am hemmed in on all sides by some of the remaining police officers – two in front of me, two behind me, and one at my side. As I carry on singing, still buzzing at the joy I am feeling, I notice small smiles and twinkling eyes appearing on the faces of my captors.

Before the van door is closed, I hear a policewoman order Sarah back to the hotel, but she is defiant and says, "No way, I am going where she is going! I am not leaving her."

This is true friendship. She will be there until the end - that is her promise to me.

With no idea of where I am being taken, and no concern of what shall happen to me once I arrive at my unknown destination, I get comfortable in my seat and continue with my song.

Leaving in the same stealth manner in which it appeared, the van exits the market square under the watchful eyes of a gathered audience. As the vehicle turns a corner, I catch a glimpse of Sarah in her wheelchair being pushed through the cobbled streets by a resigned-looking policewoman.

In what seems like less than ten minutes, I am escorted into a police station.

"You should be on the radio," a policewoman says as she leads me to a cell, making reference to the fact that I am still singing and in a world of my own.

As soon as we are in the cell, routine searches start. I am commanded to remove every item of clothing so that they can be checked for drugs – shoes, top, skirt, bra and panties – and to place each item on a narrow bench next to the policewoman. As I undress I continue singing, making song and groove out of what I am doing and loving every minute of it. It is a song that I am singing for myself (and not for my audience), this being the only way for me to fully express the way I am feeling.

My mind is in such an amazing place that nothing or nobody can bring me away from it. Even the stern expression on the policewoman's face cannot affect me because I know that here, in this cell, I can either *conform to her* mood or she can *mold to mine,* and to me, the former is not an option. If I conform to her serious and official mindset, the whole tone of the moment will change. She seeks to pull me into her charade because it is part of her role, but I'm not going there because I like where I am at. I'm not the one who is acting….she is…. because when we make eye contact I can clearly see pleasure dancing like a flame in the middle of her eyes. Therefore I am not submitting to *her* false expectations of the moment. Something tells me that this policewoman is actually enjoying my playful striptease and that she would love nothing more than to join in the fun. Anyone would. It is human nature. Happiness is infectious and everyone wants a piece of it.

When fully naked she bombards me with questions: "What is my name? Where have I been? Have I taken drugs? What am I doing in Amsterdam?"

But I do not answer her. All of these questions are irrelevant: mere distractions in an attempt to exercise some form of control over me.

"Have I got anything to say?" she asks, feigning her frustration.

"Yes, I do have something to say," I reply, light-heartedly. And then I sing, and laugh, all the time dancing along to the music that can be heard by no one but myself.

"You can take my clothes.

You can tie me down.

You can handcuff me.

And can get me to sign things and talk to me like a child.

Because it doesn't matter anymore!

I have seen beyond the *veil*.

You can take my clothes.

You can tie me down.

You can handcuff me.

And can get me to sign things and talk to me like a child.

Because it doesn't matter anymore!"

Aware that she is not going to receive the answers she has demanded the policewoman quietly leaves the cell, allowing me the solitude desired with which to go further into myself.

My insides are chanting in celebration, ecstatic at the fact that I have seen both the *veil* and the *beauty beyond it*. This presence has gently removed the covering from her face as if she is an innocent and carefree child playing a game of peek-a-boo, and her sheer presence has left me star struck......... in awe.

What's more, she has shown me that she resides in *everyone* irrespective of who they are and what role they portray in society. She is the stunning presence that I saw in Sarah, she is the hand of gentleness that I saw in the doorman, she is the twinkle in the eyes of the police officers, she is the dance in the elderly man who waltzed with me in the market square, and she is the uninhibited laughter that sprung forth from my lungs when life dared to face her with its slapstick authority. And, because of what I have seen, I know that she lives and breathes *in me*.

This Beauty is *one force*, *one presence*, *one ideal*. She transcends that which I know as the reality of life, operating above and beyond the complexities created by people and their ego charades. They do not affect her. They only affect other egos. She is totally untouched by the drama because she functions at a different level, on another plane, as though she inhabits a world that many mortal eyes do not perceive.

And with this realisation I freely submit to the Beauty *within me*, singing from the very depths of my heart a never-ending melody filled with uplifting words. Each musical note takes me into a higher state of bliss, whilst my whole body becomes the vocal chord in the throat of humanity.

And as I sing from the heart, I continue to dance........naked......moving my body to an infinite groove, as free as a butterfly that has emerged from its cocoon and taken to flight for the first time in its life.

me

ye_

naked

clothed

was

and

I was naked and ye clothed me

I was in
prison and
ye came
unto me

I
in
unto
came
was
me
ye
andprison

THE CELL I am in is unlike any that I have seen before. It is square, with a fixed bench that runs from one wall to the other. Three of its walls are bare, grey concrete (with a door in one of them), and the fourth wall is but a sheet of thick, transparent Perspex (from floor to ceiling). There is a CCTV camera in the room, positioned in an upper corner and filming my every move.

Behind the Perspex wall are stairs, probably leading to second floor offices. Police officers frequently go up and down them and, as they walk past, they stop and look in at me, as if observing a caged animal. There are no props, no luxuries, no one else in the confined space. It's just me: singing, dancing, and laughing. Does expression of such profound joy need anything more than this?

The cell door opens and a middle-aged man enters. He reminds me of a German scientist: big forehead, glasses and a serious look on his face. He orders me to sit down.

I do as he says and he sits next to me. Then he looks me in the eye, intently. "Ok, you must tell me," he says in broken English, "what have you had today? Did you take some drugs?"

"Yes I did," I reply.

"Well this reaction is not normal," he says. "Do you realise that we have the power to admit you to the psychiatric hospital?"

I nod.

"Pull yourself together!" he instructs, and then he leaves.

I stand up and continue to sing. A pumping beat comes in, so I close my eyes. The sound I am hearing is immaculate, as if it is booming forth from large, precision built speakers suspended in all four corners of the cell. There is a funky deep groove and the bass line weaves in and out of a perfect beat. I am totally absorbed in the music and can feel it infusing every cell in my body, so much so that it transports me to a spacious club, a venue comprising of a large dance floor and overhead girders upon which spotlights are suspended, their luminosity casting a multi-coloured glow over every bit of floor space.

I am dancing on a stage at the front. I turn my head to the right and see a DJ in an elevated booth about halfway between the floor and the ceiling. We make eye contact and our gazes lock. He has a big smile on his face and he gives me the thumbs up, his silent way of communicating respect for what he is witnessing. I nod and smile in return. He knows that I love every single note teeming forth from his turntables and I know that he loves the way my body is hypnotised by his choice of music, each one of us defined by the other one's groove - my song following his tunes and his tunes following my song – just pure, unadulterated appreciation tied together by a beat, a groove, and a deep knowing that something majestic is unfolding.

As the music flows, the party grows. The dance floor is heaving now with a sea of amazing faces as far as my eyes can see, as though *the veil has been removed and the Beauty has emerged from everyone here present.*

I remain on the stage, giving me all the space I need to express myself with dance. And the more I dance, the more energy I create until it is so engulfing that it touches everyone, like a massive laser beam going to thousands of hearts. I continually make eye contact with all the people on the dance floor, our smiles bonding us even deeper in recognition of the fact that they are as ecstatic as I.

It is obvious from the way we move, the way we interact, and the way we feel that we are all locked into the same vibe. The atmosphere in the place is electrifying, mind blowing, an infinite high fuelled by our feelings.

I announce to the DJ that I have declared a *state of happiness* on the whole world. He tells the crowd, and everyone cheers. You can imagine the shivers that traverse my spine as the vibrations of the combined celebratory voices hit me. Tingles start at my feet and make their way towards the top of my head, where each individual hair follicle emits its own gentle electrical shock. The hairs on my arms stand-up, and the nerve endings in my skin seem to take on a life of their own, as though they too have started to dance.

Because of the on-going cheers, whistles, and applauds, this feeling continues to heighten my senses and radiate from my body, filling everyone on the dance floor with a vibe that has never before been felt upon the face of the Earth. It's as if we have become a huge power centre, one charged with a state of happiness never before witnessed in the history of mankind.

The news of my declaration spreads around the world at the speed of lightning. I see people of all ages in cafés, bars and clubs; on the streets and in the parks; on the schoolyards and in the offices; in every country on the Earth, all sharing our vibe and freely welcoming happiness, as if they too have become part of the power centre.

And I am singing.

My voice booms all over the globe in time to the beat of the DJ. We stop and start, breaking beats and bringing in new ones, all the while cheered on by people everywhere.

Outside the cell I hear scuffles as feet move rapidly, and whispers as plans are made. I know without a doubt that TV crews have arrived and they are fighting amongst themselves as to who will interview me first. Never before has such a declaration been made upon the world. And never before have so many people embraced the song of one person in such a short space of time.

Where has this happiness come from?

Where can people get it?

They all want to know and are falling over themselves to be the first to extract the answer.

The party continues to grow, with people coming in their droves. The scene changes and I am now standing on a huge stage in what feels like a massive arena, holding hands with Nelson Mandela. Crowds sit to the left and to the right, as well as in front of us, and I recognise many famous faces in the audience. This crowd is elated; unbelievably happy.

Nelson turns and faces me, his smile beaming from ear to ear and his eyes shining like the brightest stars in a midnight sky. In a salutary manner he thrusts our clasped hands above our heads, smiling and knowing that *together we have done it!*

Liberation has come upon the world.

A State of Happiness has been forever declared......

........for people everywhere.

SEVERAL HOURS later he enters again (the German scientist) but he cannot fool me. He is with the television crew and is probably trying to prep me for the onslaught of media attention. He asks if I have thought about what he has said. *Not likely*! I reply silently.

Then he reminds me, still with a serious look upon his face, "You have a friend out there who is waiting for you or have you forgotten? She is being very patient!"

Sarah has been good to her word: *Whatever happens just be there*, and she is. She is sat right outside waiting for me.

This realisation brings me back to my immediate surroundings, to the empty grey cell with the opaque Perspex wall. My clothes are still in a bundle on the end of the bench, so I pick them up and get dressed.

I have a massive feeling of contentment in my bones, like nothing I have ever experienced before. My body is light, as if free from the effects of gravity.

I leave the cell and see Sarah in the waiting area. She too has a smile on her face, and when I come near to her she gently pinches my cheek, as a mother does to a child.

"Let me look at you," she says. "I am so pleased to see you." Her voice is motherly too, as though she is giving me the quick once over just to check that all of my features are in their correct place.

"I am so pleased to see you dressed," chirps in a policeman sitting behind a reception desk.

We all laugh, the unspoken words between us being, *it has certainly been an entertaining experience*.

"Come on, let's go," I say to Sarah.

"Yes, I think it's time," she replies.

Therefore, speak I to
them in parables

parables

Therefore

them

speak

in

to

Because

not
they see

Because they seeing see not

seeing

not hearing they

not

And hearing

And

hear

And hearing
they hear
not

understand

they

Neither do they understand

Neither

do

I REMAIN silent as we walk, listening to Sarah and her side of the day's events. It has been a wonderful afternoon for her.

She knew that I was safe – she could hear me singing – and this gave her peace of mind. She also knew that I was in good hands, my actions putting a smile on many people's faces.

"You have the body for it," she laughs. "If I had a figure like that, I would dance naked more often." We both laugh.

Sarah had sat for four hours in the waiting area. At first she was told to return to the hotel but she refused, informing the policewoman (who pushed her wheelchair) that she had a duty to me and had every intention of sticking to it. This is friendship.

Then she tells me that she had a great conversation with the police officer manning the reception desk. "I told him he should go to Blackpool... that it would open his eyes a bit!"

Blackpool is my hometown, a place with a reputation for being a tacky, Northern tourist resort. Beneath this exterior though, Blackpool has many special qualities. For those who live there, it's a town with a pulse all of its own, one whose true grandeur lies in providing a first class education in the life subjects not taught at school.

"After what I saw today," Sarah says, "Amsterdam is not *that* liberal. It is Ok so long as you stick to what they know and follow the norm, but do anything different like what you did today and it soon becomes obvious they don't quite know what to make of it."

I agree.

We are both feeling thirsty for a cold beer, so we venture into a Dutch bar situated on the corner of a cobbled street. It is near our hotel, but is not a tourist bar: it has a homely feel.

The bar man greets us and we order two beers. The heads are very frothy, taking up almost one third of the glass (which is how they are served in Holland).

Sarah and I sit at the bar with contented smiles on our faces. My respect has increased tenfold for my friend because she has shown me a new level of acceptance in the area of friendship: she did not freak out, she did not judge, and she did not become annoyed or self-centred.

She literally was.........*there, without judgement*. This is the long and short of it.

I listen as she tells me about her day, and am pleased to discover that it was the best day of the trip for her so far. She had shared her passion of tarot reading with her new acquaintance at the police station, and he was genuinely interested in what she was saying. He told her about his life in Amsterdam, and about his family and children. His English was very good.

Sarah then asks me about my experience, so I verbalise (as best as I can) the amazing feeling that engulfed me when I was dancing in the cell, and how I spearheaded a global movement of happiness. "There was a DJ playing amazing music," I say, "and cameras were linked up all over the world. Everyone was locked in to *one* groove, and it felt as though I was *the* vocal chord in the throat of the world. It was the greatest party that I have ever been to. I can still hear the music and see people's faces now."

She asks if this tells me anything.

"It does," I conclude. "It tells me that our minds are always free. They are not confined by bars or locked doors. We can be anything, and do anything, in the mind.........with our imagination. This is our liberation."

"Fascinating," she says.

I inform her that my experience was *real*. It was probably the most real experience I have ever had. Nobody could ever convince me that it was unreal because I had totally lost all attachment to my ego. It was my *real* self, the Beauty that lives *beyond the veil*, that had experienced all of these things, and nothing in the world is more real than that.

"What do you mean by *ego* and *veil*?" she asks, somewhat intrigued.

I tell Sarah about how I how saw the face of Beauty – an amazing presence housed within every individual. I share with her how the majority of people are wearing veils that hide this Beauty, the veil being a person's ego: a personality they have crafted from their limited understanding of life.

The ego is the public face for many people, meaning that the majority of their communications and interactions with others are based upon false premises. I inform Sarah that we, as a people, have become so absorbed in our personal charade – *our veiled perception of life* – that we have forgotten who we are and what the true purpose of our life actually is.

"Today I saw it," I reminisce, with a broad smile on my face. "It was pure Beauty – an amazing presence – a power - residing at the very centre of everyone, and it totally eclipsed the role that they were *trying* to portray to me. I saw it in you, Sarah: you are not disabled. I saw it in the doorman: there was nothing tough about him. I saw it in the police officers. I saw it in everybody whom I made eye contact with."

"What did you see?"

"In you I saw a stunning female presence with the most beautiful, serene, and joyous face I have ever seen. After I witnessed her in you, I saw her personality in everyone else that I made eye contact with, as though she lives *within* all of us. All we need to do, as individuals, is give her her freedom of expression, as in let her come out and take her place in the world. When we do this, she will take us to places that we can't even conceive with our limited mode of thinking; with our conditioned egos.

All those dreams, those ideals, and those wonderful moments you think about when daydreaming.......this is her, Sarah. She has a *perfect plan for you*. She knows the role that you are to play in the world – not just in *your* narrow vision of life – but in *her great scheme* of living and evolution. She's seeking her manifestation in the world, through you. All you have to do is *acknowledge and accept her*, and it starts by removing the veil of ego from her face, not just for a brief moment, but for a lifetime. When you do this, your most *ideal life* – that is, *the ultimate vision of good in life that you could possibly imagine for you* – becomes your reality. She is *that* beautiful and unique!"

I pause and sip on my beer, watching as Sarah ponders on the things that I am saying to her. Even though we come from very different social and cultural backgrounds, we have always found it easy to talk to each other about anything, and this is why we have become good friends.

I resume our conversation. "When I say that you are not disabled, I am meaning that there is *nothing disabled about the Beauty within you*. This inner presence, this power, is not affected by any of your physical attributes because it is already *whole and complete*. She contains a perfect plan for your life – one that will bring you all the happiness and joy you could ever hope and wish for - meaning that your so-called disability is *essential to her*.

Sarah, you have lived, mentally, in your physical disability for so long that you are living your own man-made lie. Whenever you have urges to do things, the first thoughts that dominate are those that say you *can't* because you are disabled, causing you to fear something that could potentially be good for you. You allow your ego to govern everything you do, and this prevents you from positively moving forward in life, which in turn enhances your feelings of frustration, confusion, jealousy, failure, and many other self defeating traits. It's a downward spiral into everything that doesn't bring you happiness. Don't you see?"

"I do see," she agrees. "It is quite something to take in. I know that if I'd have listened to others about coming to Amsterdam, I would never have gotten on the plane even though my heart told me that everything would be fine. This trip is turning out to be one of the best times of my life."

"I'll drink to that," I respond, raising my glass.

We toast the occasion, and then order a refill.

"Sarah, do you realise that today you ran? I have never seen you move so quick!"

She giggles. "Yeah, it felt good. I didn't think I had it in me."

"It's because you gave no thought to your disability. You gave it no attention. You felt young, excited, and adventurous. Don't you see?

The doorman! He didn't want to be angry or annoyed......it is not his *true* nature, and yet his man-made lie told him that he *had* to be angry and annoyed, therefore showing himself to be nothing more than a puppet straddling the hand of ego.

I find it bizarre Sarah. At what point in our lives did we choose to give our power over to the ego? Why don't we choose to let Beauty manifest in our lives? Is it because nobody knows she exists, or are we deliberately ignoring her?"

I ORDER another beer for each of us, watching silently as the bar tender levels off the froth. He smiles and asks if we are enjoying our stay in Amsterdam.

"Yes, you could say that!" grins Sarah.

We both smoke and look around, enjoying another silent moment.

"There is something of extreme importance here," I say to her, "because now I am faced with the one and only question: *What do I do from this moment forward?* Do I give my life over to the ideal of Beauty contained within me – just as I did today - or do I continue letting my ego dictate how my life is going to unfold?"

"I know what I'd like to do," she replies, "but what does it mean and what does it involve? I don't think I have witnessed her like you, and I am certainly not ready to eat a box of Philosopher's Truffles just to find out."

Her comment makes me laugh. "To be honest, I don't know what it means for us," I reply, "for me, for you, for anybody else. All I know is that I am living the illusion just like everyone else. I have done everything I am *conditioned* to do in terms of career, education, all that sort of stuff, but it doesn't mean that it feels right or that it *is* right for that matter. If it was, I wouldn't feel so disillusioned with life! I think that I stay on this routine treadmill because I don't know what the alternative is. It's like we are all just repeating what others have done before because nobody really knows if there is another way that leads to complete fulfillment in life."

"And you believe that what you have experienced today *is the alternative*?" asks Sarah, sincerely.

"I do! Pure Beauty is here Sarah. This I know for sure. And she never goes away. She is always residing within, locked up until we find the key and decide to set her free. She will call to you, whisper your name, and even enter your dreams, but the decision to open the door - to remove the veil from her face - is yours and yours alone.

She won't force or coerce you into living the *ideal and joyous life* that she has planned for you. She will simply let you be until you realise that there is more to life than what you have previously known. Then, when you start searching for the key to life, to love, to happiness and joy - to *all the goodness that you know exists in this world* – then she will show her face. Her beauty is eternal.....it doesn't age or grow tired and weary; it doesn't fade with the changing tides of life because her presence is the silent anchor of life, one that, once cast, enables you to sail confidently through the roughest of seas.

But what I want to know is this: How do we bring her to the forefront of our lives without mind-altering drugs?"

Sarah shakes her head. "I don't know. I really don't."

"How do we live, every day, without our ego veils, free from the tiring charade of mediocrity?" I ask. "How do we invite the inner power – Beauty - *into* our life, all of the time, 24-7, so that she is *leading* and *driving* our individual lives? Sarah, I must find the answer because, when I do, I have a duty to let others know. This experience happened to me today for a reason and I cannot just file it away as being but a mere moment of madness.

Today she made herself known to *me*. She showed me *her* face.

And when I submitted to her, I experienced *her* ways......her Vision for humankind.

And it was glorious. It was beautiful.

Not just for me, but for everybody in the whole world."

profit

woman a
         it

what   For what shall it
   For   profit a woman   shall

the
gain
If
whole
shall
If she shall gain
the whole world
she
world

lose
But
soul
her

own

But lose her own soul

WE DEPART from Amsterdam a couple of days later. Sarah returns to Eastbourne and I to Blackpool. When I get back to my daily routine I feel different, knowing that a permanent change has taken place in me.

As I recall details of my incarceration to family and friends, they laugh by imagining the escapade playing itself out. But, underneath the humour, I know that I am now presented with the mission of finding the missing key - one which does not rely on Class A's, Class B's or Class C's. It is a task which I struggle to verbalise to others except my six-year old nephew. Possessing the eyes of a child, he shows understanding where the majority of adults fail.

What makes the goal ahead seem difficult is the fact that I don't really know where to start, nor do I have any idea of where the road will lead. I am walking midway between nothing and everything, the adventure being the discovery of a long lost treasure that has no common name.

Or...........maybe it does! In Amsterdam I readily related the ego to life's lie, so perhaps the Beauty within is more commonly known as its opposite, and is therefore called Truth. Yes, the Beauty of Truth, or Beautiful Truth, this is the treasure that I believe I am searching for.

But how do I convey this?

If I asked people to point me to the grand illusion of life – to *the lie* - they would rapidly reel off a long list of names and situations (both past and present). This would prove an easy task for them because everyone seems to carry grudges for a person or a situation in which they believe they have been duped or taken for a fool.

Asking someone to point me to the Truth though is a different concept all together.

I imagine myself talking to an assistant at the local tourist information bureau, saying *Hey! Can you tell me where Truth is?*

I ask my mum for directions. She does not know.

I ask my sister. She just tells me to chill-out and skin-up.

I ask my boss if he has any idea. He laughs and replies, *4pm on a Friday*.

The people I question seem to think it is my new punch line, a continuation of my Amsterdam experience, and it soon grows old.

When I make an effort to chat about my insight into the ego and the veil, the same people roll their eyes - at the ceiling if they are on their own and at others if there is company.

A colleague summed it up perfectly when he said to me: *Maybe you should go away again*

*for a few days so that you have a different story
to talk about.*

But the feeling, the impact, and the
revelation - they do not go away. They stay with
me and grow stronger every day, like a hot coal
burning right into my chest. I notice that when I
look at people, I see *beyond their veil*, intuitively
recognising their Beauty within. I see nothing but
her, as though the *clarity of vision* and the
potential of our relationship have remained with
me.

If deceit rears its head, I see honesty
standing tall behind it. And if depression takes
over, I behold joy dancing behind the tears.

Because I know, more than at any other
time in my life, that everything on the surface
isn't real. It's just an illusion - the ego's master-
lie - which everyone is unwittingly playing along
with, as though they are mesmerised by the
discordant melodies of the Pied Piper.

My gratitude towards Sarah feels infinite.
She showed me that the extent of her disabilities
weren't real: they do not exist but in the realm of
the ego, and it is this that breathes life into them,
like a wooden puppet she has been intent on
turning into a real little girl.

Whatever we choose to focus on with the
limited vision of the ego (a vision *restricted* by

the intellectual wardrobe of materialism, formality, prejudice and cultural expectations), eventually manifests itself in every aspect of our life - good or bad, positive or negative, right or wrong, fact or fiction.

And so whenever anyone moans, or grumbles, or talks about the bad hand they have been dealt, I cannot believe it. I refuse to.

Because inside of their skin *is* everything they could ever want in life: Greatness. Liberation. Joy. Love. Unity. Beauty, and everything else that brings them true happiness.

This does not change. *It is*. And always will be. It can be no different. For it is what it is.

It is Truth. The Beautiful Truth of life.

Truth is eternal. It is fixed and will go forth through generations until the end of time. We only need to look at mathematical Truths to verify this. One plus one will always equal two, whether we do the addition now or five thousand years from this date.

The Law of Gravity will always remain. It doesn't change because our desires in life change or society's expectations alter. The Law of Gravity is unchanging and we work with it....again, and again, and again.....because it is a *Truth*. We cannot work against it because it is Universal Law, applicable to everyone and everything, irrespective of who, what, and where they are.

And this is what I am talking about now.

Beauty and her ideal is Truth – a *Universal Power (or Force) bound by a fixed law that underpins all of Life* – meaning that we must work *with* it.....with her.

Doing this results in *every good thing* that we could ever wish for in our lives. All the effects that we seek in our desperate attempt to build an amazing, happy life is already in our hand, it is just that we allow the ego and its attention-seeking charades to distort our perception and therefore interfere with the perfect execution of Beautiful Truth in our lives, the result being more toil and less inner peace.

Ask anyone what an *ideal life* means to them, and they will tell you without even a pause for thought because it is *written on their hearts*, as though they are already pre-programmed with it. The perfect plan for *their life* is already contained within them, just as the blueprint for an oak tree is contained within *its* seed. Everyone's ideal (and beautiful) life is unique to them, meaning that its outcome is assured if its possibility is truly believed in.

But the thing which alludes me is my task of finding the solution to all of this, because

I know that it is only when I have discovered the solution can the problem be revealed to others. Like a master scientist I could theorise until grey hairs sprout from my head, but this is likely to fall on deaf ears because people want results!

We are the results driven generation.

We don't want theory. The ego wants practical application – good, old, tried and tested practical application. Only then, when the results are in front of people - in black and white with some shades of blood - will I be taken seriously.

And so I ask myself, without answer, where is the key for which I search, that which brings forth Beauty into every day living by permanently removing the veil from her face and eliminating me from the clutches of ego?

I know, without a shadow of a doubt, that I want to *feel* the same as I did in Amsterdam every single day of my life: the freedom that consumed me, the sudden ability I possessed which enabled me to *see through* the charade without being affected by it, and the natural inclination to laugh at it all - this all felt so good to me and, like an addict, I want it every day. It's how life is to be lived. This I know for sure.

And the music that I heard! It's beat pumped through my veins, booming from speakers not crafted by man's own hands, it's very melody urging me to dance, dance, dance......a simple act that brought everyone together and spread the vibe of happiness throughout the world quicker than humanity has ever known before.

I appreciate that all of this sounds idealistic, but this is a judgement of the ego, that which is *limited by the physical appearance* of things. Even though this is the common way of thinking in society, it is still a *contradiction of Truth*, with daily evidence showing it as the cause of all hardship, suffering, and confusion in life.

Why else are the majority of people suspended in a state of lack and want, of struggle and distaste for what they see in the world? It is because we are bombarded by the actions of ego personalities, the consequences thrust in our faces every day, dragging each and every one of us into a drama we have come to accept as life. Look at the ridiculous way people acted in Amsterdam. Since when has a riot van of armed officers ever been deployed to detain a laughing and singing female?

The thing is, I know that life doesn't have to be this way – for me or for anybody else. I admit that I too have been an unwitting (albeit active) participant in this global comedy -

memorising lines, enacting parts, and seeking acceptance from a faceless audience – all in the name of conforming to an unspoken and yet very loud-mouthed norm of life.

But now, because of what I have seen and experienced first hand, I know that I can make a conscious choice to live my life in a *different way,* from a *different perspective and vantage point.* I have been offered a shot at life like nothing ever presented to me before, the opportunity being the certainty that everything I have ever conceived as being an amazing life is within arm's reach to me and is mine if I believe in its possibility. Nobody can withhold this life from me because it doesn't come from without. It is only by denying its surety that it is withheld.

I want to remove the veil that separates me from my good...from my ideal. I want to live my life with Beautiful Truth at the forefront of everything I do. She has shown me that she is alive, that she is real, and that she is ready for me to invite her into the world.

And I do want this.

I long to feel her, to taste her, and to be her, everyday.

But how?

For she that seeketh, findeth

knocketh
be
that
To
shall
opened
ither

And to her that knocketh
it shall be opened

NOT TOO long after, a colleague who I haven't spoken to before sits next to me at lunchtime.

Whilst eating I generally don't tend to converse (I like to focus on my food and taste what I am putting into my mouth), hence I do not make any audible greetings or informal gestures to signal to him that the dialogue highway is open. I simply offer a polite nod of acknowledgement.

He smiles at me and says, "Hello, I'm Michael."

"Hello, I'm Joanne," I reply, courteously.

"I know. I have seen you before. You work in engineering don't you?"

I turn and look at him, making eye contact. He has a gentle face and, for the first time since my trip, I see *no veil*. I look deeper into his eyes and, taken aback, see that which I have been looking for. He has it! I can clearly see it, because his inwards are the same as his outwards. There is no second personality hiding in the dark under the shadow of the ego! His Beautiful Truth is out in the open for everyone to see.

"Yes. And you?" I reply.

"Art."

"Oh, interesting," I say. "What sort of art?"

"Painting...acrylics mainly. Personally I like abstract stuff but I have to teach what's on the syllabus."

"Yeah, I know the feeling! Most of the syllabus' I teach were written ten years ago. Not exactly cutting edge for tomorrow's engineer is it?"

Michael smiles. "You can see some of my personal paintings in the new contemplation room at the front of the college. There are two pieces on display in there."

"I will pop along and have a look. Gives me a good excuse to go and check out the new décor. What are they of?" I enquire sincerely.

"One is of Truth, and the other of Light," he replies, still smiling.

"How do you paint Truth?" I ask, surprised. "I have a hard time finding it, never mind painting it."

"That's a funny statement," he responds. "You don't need to look for Truth."

We sit for a long time, and I share with him my Amsterdam experience. His eyes twinkle as he listens, and then he says that he has had the same experience although it was not through drugs.

He has arrived a different way.

"In conclusion," he says, "any man can live in the Truth by simply asking Jesus Christ to *reveal* it in their life."

I swallow hard and momentarily lose eye contact with him, wondering whether I have simply opened the flood gates for a lunch time preaching session. This is not what I was expecting......

Bible bashers,

Fanatical religious nuts,

People singing monotone in church whilst waving their hands at the ceiling!

This is *not* cool.

"That's the key to the door within", says Michael. "He is the Truth. He is the Way. He is that which you are searching for."

And with nothing more to add, Michael gets up from the table and leaves, just like when the policeman opened the door to the cell and I walked out.

EVIDENCE speaks for itself, and Michael is *happy*. Genuinely happy! His eyes ooze with it, like ice cream dripping from a baby's chin. In addition to this, he is the only person I have met since my trip who has provided an actual solution to my search, even if it does sound foreign to my ears.

Admittedly he is not singing and dancing naked in the student canteen, but maybe, just maybe, my naked dancing experience is but a wonderful metaphor of something much, much greater, this metaphor being that the Beauty I witnessed and submitted myself to is actually *the naked Truth in all of its glory*. She has nothing to hide, nothing to learn, and also nothing to fear because she *has it all* already.

She is not clothed in layers of doubt or prejudice like the ego.

She does not wear mental make-up to camouflage deep-rooted scars that hinder her growth.

And she is not housed in the latest verbal accessory just to make herself feel important.

In her purest form, she is the most fascinating force of beauty that we will ever witness in our lifetime, and she is a power that resides in each and every person.

This is the Truth of life….the Beautiful Truth of life.

There are many pieces of art in the world that have a mesmerising effect on its observer, as though the artist used a brush named Immaculate Expression. Critics and non-critics alike can find only pleasure in these pieces, whilst millions of pounds are used to ensure that they are preserved to time indefinite, as though perfect beauty and the possession of it is an obsession of the world.

Some art collectors purchase these pieces (if they are available) and see investment only, wrapping them up and storing them in vaults far away from the eyes of the appreciative. The collector may not care for the inherent value of artistic expression…..only the trading financial statement is of any concern…..and this is what Beautiful Truth has become to humanity in its desperation to evolve.

The *real essence of true and lasting happiness*, that which everybody craves in life, is locked away in people's *own personal dungeon of ignorance*, whilst they trade themselves for as much (or as little) as they can get. Unbeknown to them, their hidden canvas portrays a vision of life that is more colourful than any painting one person's brush could ever create, and is more priceless than any financial value another person could ever put on it.

It's as if we are saying to the fabulous artwork tucked *within*, that we would rather have the shabby cloth it is wrapped in than the real masterpiece this material covers.

In the cell I was shown the true purpose of life: *To remove the veil from the face of Beautiful Truth.*

Therefore, this means that the only duty for me in *my* lifetime is to dismiss the ego and unleash *my* naked Truth on the world, this Truth being that which leads to the *manifestation of an ideal and beautiful life* as *contained within me*, and one which *benefits the whole world*.

they see your see eyes

Blessed are your eyes, for they see

are

Blessed

for

ears
they for

And

hear

And your ears,

your

for they hear.

FOR A couple of days following my conversation with Michael, I do nothing. I simply play with his suggestion, turning it over in my mind, whilst trying to gauge how I feel about the solution he has presented.

This is the first time the notion of Jesus Christ has entered my sphere of existence – at least as an adult anyway. Religious Education teachers at school taught me to copy out, word for word, sections of the Bible for examination purposes, but this was more of an exercise in memorising as opposed to understanding (a popular technique used to secure top grades).

My circle of friends and my general lifestyle don't bring me into contact with anybody whom is into the Jesus thing. Holistic therapies like massage, Reiki, acupuncture - anything classed as *alternative* - is more normal to me. But Jesus Christ? Even the mere thought of mentioning his name to others makes me feel uncomfortable. Why, I cannot say. I just know that he is very alien to me and is part of a world that has no common thread with mine.

And so, during these few days, I question and analyse how I truly feel, having some concern over what it may mean.

Thoughts of churches and other religious groups don't gel with me. I am not into cliques because many times they are a breeding ground for gossip and prejudices, something that tends to go hand-in-hand with the organised religion territory.

Because of my diverse and open-minded background, acceptance of others is a quality that has become a natural part of my character, and this is something that I am not willing to forego in order to fit in with the mentality of a specific group.

I certainly can't take Michael's advice easily, but the one factor which keeps hitting home to me - *the lowest common denominator in it all* - is this: *he wears no veil, he is happy, and he has offered a solution* (the only person whom has). Surely this should be the fundamental basis upon which I form my decision as to whether or not I accept his recommendation.

Ask Jesus Christ to *reveal the Truth* in my life? Ok, let's give it a go.

If I was willing to put a full box of Philosophers Truffles down my throat for a new experience, then asking this Saviour of the World to come into my life is easy. It's only words, right?

And so I do.

And nothing happens.

Until about ten days later.

I AM walking to work, not really wanting to go but feeling duty bound to do so. It is the same route, same corners, same road that I travel every day.

When I reach a familiar turning point I hear an authoritative voice in my head, which says, "All is Forgiven Now."

It is so clear, loud, and real that I stop in my tracks - semi-paralysed. Moments later a massive load seems to dissolve from my shoulders. I am not talking about something the size of a small backpack. No, this is more like a giant iceberg that suddenly evaporates into thin air.

As the weight leaves my body, I feel my whole posture rebalance, and it dawns on me how much negativity, for want of a better word, has set-up camp around my neck without me even realising that it was there.

This experience lasts just a few seconds but, in this brief moment, every bit of guilt, anxiety, worry and burden – anything which has plagued my mind throughout my life – literally just leaves, as if to say, *These are all gone now. Think of them no more. They are of no relevance.*

I know this is Jesus Christ. It is too unique to be anything other than his voice.

Aware that I am still standing in the street, gobsmacked by what has just happened, I continue walking, this time at a much slower pace and in total awe. I even look around to see if anybody else has just experienced the same thing as me but I am the only person on the pavement.

As I walk the voice speaks to me again, and says "Are you willing to give your whole life to me?"

I say, humbly & slightly embarrassed, "Yes. Yes I am."

What else could I say?

And then the silence follows.

THIS SILENCE continues for around ten days more, however there appears to be a series of coincidences occurring in my life, especially with regards work, the one environment I feel very out of sync with.

Perhaps this is Truth showing itself via outside circumstances, or maybe it is the lie showing itself, because the words *what you see without are but a reflection of what is within* hit me harder than they ever have before.

I am teaching a class on meditation to a group of people with functional mental health issues, namely depression, stress and other such conditions. Because of my enthusiasm for meditation, I had devised a course and offered it to colleagues as part of a workplace development programme. Due to the successful outcome of this course, it was then proposed that I deliver it to adults in the community, and this is our second meeting.

As I am talking to the adult learners about meditation and the way we can creatively use our imagination to bring about positive change in our lives, I notice that one woman is sitting with a blank expression on her face, another is wearing a smile but with hopelessness shielding her eyes, and a third woman is dozing off to sleep. Like a bandage being ripped from my eyes, I suddenly ask myself, *is this what I want from life? Do I want to be spending my days looking out at desolate and lost faces such as these?*

Immediately I answer No, and then I question, *what does this say about me?*

On a second occasion during this ten-day period, I am teaching a group of engineering students when the same *what-does-this-say about-me* insight hits me again. Many of the students are raising a fuss about the syllabus, asking questions as to why they need to learn some of the topics. I explain to them that the topics are a fundamental part of the curriculum (a conversation we have had on several occasions), but no amount of logical reasoning fulfills their want for an answer, the unspoken reason being that they prefer the qualification without putting in the effort required to attain the standard.

As I am talking, I stop mid-sentence, suddenly realising that I am using the same words, the same reasons, and the same cycle of spoon-fed knowledge that I have used since commencing work in Further Education nearly a decade ago. And then, just like before, it immediately dawns on me that *this is not what I want* from my life.

This isn't my idea of teaching. It never was. It never will be. So therefore, *whom am I fooling?*

The third realisation is in the staff room. I am sitting eating lunch, listening to my colleagues as they moan and complain about everything they can possibly moan and complain about. During the lunchtime break it is a common occurrence for this collective of professionals to embrace the woes of the world, assigning themselves as martyrs to its cause.

Not wanting to get involved in the futile conversation, I ask myself, *what is wrong with them all. Are their lives really so sad?*

And then it hits me, full on in the face, right between the eyes, like an invisible fist reigning down from the sky, BANG, BANG, BANG, and I realise it isn't them!

It isn't the students.

It isn't the staff.

It isn't the sad faces.

It is *me*!

Me, me, ME!

I am in this situation and their company, not because of anything wrong with them, but because I am the *exact* example of the lie I had discovered and seen with my own eyes in Amsterdam. What my life is showing me here and now, in black and white, is just how far in the deceit I have actually come.

Removing another layer off my veil, I put my half-eaten sandwich on the desk and pick my coat up off the back of a chair. Without saying a word or making eye contact with anyone, I walk out – first from the staff room....and then from the building - knowing that in this moment I am leaving it all behind, literally shutting the door on an existence I have spent my whole life creating.

I walk the same route home, but this time I do not recognise anything because my dialogue - my observation - is inside. Yes, it is inside.

In a pathetic, last-ditch, feeble attempt to control the situation (but knowing it is well beyond my reach), I mentally tantrum like a child and shout at Jesus Christ, "You win! I'm done! Finished! I cannot do it my way anymore!"

Picking up this tormented inner child between my thumb and forefinger, I toss her towards him like a piece of waste paper, her body falling in a heap at his feet. "There you go," I yell as I walk away. "Take her, she's yours. I don't want her anymore. She isn't my responsibility. Do with her what you will!"

FOR A couple of days I loiter around the house, having no inclination to speak with anyone or to go anywhere. By the third day brutal honesty has been frank with me, and the question of *what is it that I want to do with my life?* - as in really want - has been answered.

My passion has always been for writing, with my ideal work focus in life being that of an author. I love taking walks and contemplating life, noting down observations, thoughts, and feelings. Notebooks filled with poems, part finished stories, and my general observations line several shelves in my home, this being an on going drive to nurture my writing talent. It is obvious from recent happenings that the moment to embrace this deep yearning of mine is upon me now.

I decide to take a vacation, picturing a backpacking journey to Spain armed with a laptop and my newfound awareness. With a mental postcard of my destination, I go to the local travel agents, the aim being to collect holiday brochures for reference.

Whilst browsing their offerings, an agent asks if I would like any assistance. I tell her that I am fine (assuming she will then go away) but she enquires as to what sort of holiday I am looking for.

I inform her that I am thinking of going to Spain for a short break, possibly leaving in the next few days, and she says, in a very helpful tone, "Let me see what I have got on the system."

Because of her friendly (and persistent) nature, I decide to sit down and let her assist.

"I have a flight leaving for Los Angeles tomorrow morning," she says. "It is at a very good price."

"Los Angeles? What is there?" I ask.

"Oh, it is a fantastic city. There is so much to see and do," she replies, enthusiastically.

"Like what?" I enquire.

"There are stunning beaches, for example Malibu Beach. There is Hollywood, and Beverley Hills. I love Los Angeles," she says with a broad smile. "It's great."

"Sounds interesting. Will I be safe travelling on my own?"

"Oh yes, you will be fine."

"What is the weather like at this time of year?"

"It's probably very similar to Spain. Mainly sunshine with most days being nice and hot."

I purchase a three-month flight ticket and arrange for a taxi to collect me at the crack of dawn the next morning. My heart is beating fast, but I am not scared. Inside I am telling myself that I am ready to *put it all to the test*: to observe how the Beautiful Truth actually works on a day-to-day basis.

I am willing to trust in her, and to give her the freedom to express *her ideal* through me however she chooses. I am eager to go with her flow, and to be led in my every step without my own ego-driven, pre-packaged or ready made plans. And should this approach to life cause me to fall flat on my face, then at least I have had the courage to take the chance...........to *open the door and set her free*!

When one witnesses the majesty of the Beauty within like I have, followed by a commanding voice that asks, *Are you willing to give your life to me?*, then in reality there is no other alternative but to embrace that which lies before me.

As I stand at the crossroads of life, I see in front of me two potential routes. One charts the way to *Mediocrity*, continuing on in the same way as before and playing by the *man-made* rules and regulations that I have been *conditioned* to conform to. It is a busy, wide road with people walking in all directions, similar to a parade of headless chickens.

The other leads me to a destination called an *Ideal and Beautiful Life*. It is a narrow, winding road, upon which just a few people walk, all going in the same direction.

People on the wide road look agitated, and frustrated, as though they are frightened to stop for just one moment. Those on the narrow road look happy and deeply content, with joyful expectation, love, and acceptance in their eyes. They walk at a much slower pace than those on the wide road, as though their arrival is assured.

With my flight ticket in hand, I start off along the narrow road. My first stopping point is my credit card phone line, transferring ten thousand pounds into my bank account. The next stop is an electrical goods store where I invest in a laptop and carry case. With just a few hours of the day left, I pack my belongings and put household business in order.

Due to the attitude of friends and family, I know that my trip is to be kept incognito. Even though they don't mean to, people can easily prevent you from doing things because of the fears *they* have in life (like discouraging Sarah from going Amsterdam). Because this journey is about *my* understanding of Beautiful Truth, I know that the only way to go is by telling no one.

By fully relying on the presence which is *inside me,* and by acutely observing how she functions and communicates with me, then (and only then) will I truly understand her methods of expression on a day-to-day basis. When I have this knowledge, based on raw experience, then I can confidently and honestly inform others about her potential.

As part of my departure preparations I write four letters, each with the same, short message: *By the time you read this I shall be on a plane. I have decided to go away for a few months. Do not worry. I will be in touch. I love you.*

When the sun relieves the moon from its night duty, I drop the letters into the post box and get into the taxi. I have no map, no accommodation, no tourist guide, and no idea as to my destination. But this is fine, because the powerful urge and my belief in what I am doing will take me to the right places.

As the taxi makes it way to the airport, I affirm to myself that *I will not fear, for fear feeds the lie.*

All I know is that the journey ahead of me shall unfold one moment at a time and, as it does, I will capture it with my pen, this being my personal way of feeding and clothing the

Beautiful Truth because, by doing this, the Beautiful Truth and her promises will feed and clothe me.

Come unto
me, all ye
that labour all
unto that
Come
me

And are heavy laden

And I
will give ye rest

give

rest will

I And ye

I NEED a comfortable bed. I am tired. It has been a long flight.

As the escalator carries me down to the main arrivals area of LAX airport, I see a large red notice board with the word ACCOMMODATION emblazoned across the top.

Looking at the posted listings nothing really catches my eye, the majority of offerings being B&B's and private telephone numbers. Because I am in need of sleep, the last thing that I want to do is converse with a stranger at the end of a phone line in the hope of finding a suitable bed in a city that I know nothing about.

Affirming that *all is good*, I scan the arrivals area and see an information kiosk. As I walk towards it, I pass a cameraman filming a female as she speaks into a microphone. On the plane I had read an article that described L.A. as being the world's largest film set, and already, without leaving the airport, I have debuted my first walk-on part.

I also find it amusing that, following my insight into every day actors performing on life's stage, I have been brought half way across the world to a location that is noted for its life *in front* of the lens.

The assistant at the kiosk is helpful. She can arrange one night for $40 in a five star hotel, situated just minutes from the airport. It has a swimming pool, spa, and everything I need for a comfortable stay. A shuttle bus leaves the airport every fifteen minutes and will drop me directly at the hotel lobby.

In less than an hour I am sat in the rooftop jacuzzi, its bubbles massaging my skin like a lullaby gracefully teasing the ears. Tired but relaxed, I am both pleased and relieved to have found such perfect accommodation on my first day here. However I wouldn't expect anything less because of the way I am *trusting* in my Beautiful Truth, accepting that all which comes into my life from now on is essential to her optimum and perfect unfolding. She knows what I like, and it is this that I am trusting in.

Trusting: This is the word of the moment for me.

The heat of the sun pummels my face, and a smell of freshly cooked breakfast lingers around my nostrils. Every now and then I open my eyes and look out across the L.A. skyline, seeing rooftops and buildings, all the while thinking *I have done it. I am here.*

A man and woman climb into the jacuzzi. We start to chat. They ask if I am enjoying my stay in L.A., so I inform them that I have just arrived. The man explains how they are on their way home having spent a week in the city, and then he enquires about my plans. When he knows that I don't have a specific itinerary, he suggests that the beach should be my first stopping point.

"The location you are in now is very industrial," he says. "These hotels are mainly airport stopovers. I can show you on a map if you like. We won't need it anymore."

"Yes, I would like that," I reply.

He reaches over to his bag and withdraws a crumpled city map and a pen. Unfolding a large section of it, he moves closer to me so that I can see the map too. "This is where you should go," he says, circling an area in black ink. "It is a great place to start your trip."

"Yes, I agree," says the female at his side. "It is very lively, lots going on, you will enjoy it there."

"Ok, I will take your advice, and thanks." Half an hour later I am lying on the bed in the hotel room, flicking through channels on the TV, the majority of which are showing either news or adverts.

Being on the tenth floor I have views across the city. The sun is high in the sky and its rays reflect off the multitude of windows. A summer haze hangs loosely over the buildings, like an eagle gliding across the land.

In the room there is a large executive desk upon which I place my laptop, the aim being to type an account of my journey so far. However, when I switch the computer on, I notice that its charge is less than ten percent. It also dawns on me that I do not have the appropriate voltage adapter to plug into the mains (a necessity if I am to successfully write about my adventure as it unfolds). With this in mind, I switch the computer off and set the acquisition of the correct adapter as a priority for the next day.

Top of my list right now though is sleep. Anything to do with tomorrow is being sent packing with an overnight bag and, having waved it off at the platform, I close my eyes and enter into a deep, long, sleep.

The next day I wake early, very early, maybe four a.m. early. In my handbag are sandwiches from the flight, so I eat these and make a cup of tea, after which I take out my notebook and write a short diary.

Mother comes to mind and I wonder if she has received her letter, however I do not dwell on the question, choosing instead to give no more thought to it. In the scheme of things, I know that time will aid her understanding of why I had to get on the plane, leaving everything and everyone behind.

Initially she may feel saddened and confused by my actions, but this too will subside with time. All I know is that this journey cannot accommodate the worry or concerns of other people. It is a lesson – my lesson - in learning to work with the inner power of Beauty, something which may sound strange if I were to openly talk of it.

Some critics would likely say that I am selfish, some would say I am stupid, whilst others wouldn't be interested at all, at least not at this stage of the journey anyway. These reactions don't bother me though, because these were the general attitudes that were shown to the Wright Brothers when they took to the sky in a wooden bird back in 1903. Who would have thought that the early efforts of these brothers would define a whole industry and a new lifestyle opportunity for people?

If anybody is seeking to do things a different way - to push the boundaries in any field of endeavour - then they have to be willing to submit themselves *wholeheartedly* to their inner knowing, even when those around them advise contrary to this knowing. This is what I am doing.

Galileo was found guilty of heresy, spending his lifetime under house arrest because of his theory that the Earth and other planets revolve around the Sun. Now he is championed as someone who played a major role in the Scientific Revolution, as though those who sanctioned his confinement now *embrace his genius*.

Socrates, who once said that *there exists an ideal world above and beyond the world of matter*, is credited as being one of the founders of Western philosophy. However, in his lifetime, he was accused of corrupting the youth of Athens, and of impiety (of not believing in the many gods of the State but in one God). Found guilty at trial of these two counts, his punishment was a nice cocktail of lethal poison, another example of how a person is at first condemned and then (when the rest of the world catches up) elevated as one of the greatest minds in history.

It is easy to write off my comparison and say, *hey, but we're talking about Galileo and Socrates here*. This I know. But I am also certain that that which has been revealed to me is essential to the evolutionary progress of humanity.

Beautiful Truth showed me that she exists in each and every one of us, therefore it is to the *benefit of all* that a *clear understanding of her methods of expression* is attained. I am convinced of this so deeply that I am willing to surrender my whole life to this quest.

LOS ANGELES is home to the Hollywood sign, so I make a visit to this the aim of the morning.

At eight o'clock I check out of the hotel and walk to a car hire place, stopping at the first one I see. Within twenty minutes I am navigating the USA highways in a brand new, sporty white car, complete with spoilers, sound system, and large sunroof.

Windows are down and the music is loud. On rotation in the CD player is *Funkdust*, a track I produced as a *thank you* gift to both the house music scene (for the fantastic memories it has given me over the years), and also to the DJ who partnered me all night long in the Amsterdam police cell.

Whenever I hear *Funkdust,* a vivid scene comes to mind, one that I painted as I composed the track. In this scene I am dressed in a pair of shorts, a figure hugging T-shirt, and my platform dancing shoes. Strung across my body is a small shoulder bag filled with gold dust – *Funkdust* - and I dance across the rooftops of the world sprinkling this dust.

When the *Funkdust* lands on people – on their heads, their faces, and their shoulders – they experience profound happiness and start dancing. It is a dance of their Beautiful Truth......of the majesty of their inner self. The happiness they emit infects all who cast their eyes upon them, causing others to dance too, until everyone is grooving to the silent music of the world.

With a smile on my face and the music booming in my ears, I enjoy an easy drive along the main road towards Hollywood. Every time nerves show themselves, I affirm my trust and order them to *be gone*. Fear isn't what this trip is about.

The Beautiful Truth is that *I am exactly where I am meant to be*.

Traffic is slow, starting and stopping, giving me a chance to take in the surroundings. The road I am on leads me past a very vibrant district. Buildings, cafes, and shops.....they look full of life! And one building in particular grabs my attention.

It is colourful and imposing, on a corner near the beach. My eyes are drawn to it immediately, causing me to question: *what is the name of this area?*

But I continue, my blinkered goal being to reach the Hollywood sign.

THE HOLLYWOOD sign and Chicago are the only places that have held any appeal to me in America. Chicago, due to it being the birthplace of house music; and the Hollywood sign because it is like a childhood friend, one that I got to know during my relationship with the TV. In fact the States has never been on my radar as a continent I would like to visit, and hence my knowledge of this vast country is somewhat limited.

Both Chicago and the Hollywood sign have, in their own unique way, made their presence known to me, rather than me discovering them via a travel guide, and it is for this reason that I feel an affiliation with them.

It is similar to my experience with Beautiful Truth, in that *she made herself known to me* in her own unique way. Jesus Christ did the same, in that he came forward as the solution to my unknown. He was the one who virtually said, *it is through me that a permanent connection is made,* even if the words were spoken via Michael's mouth.

En-route to the sign I drive up Sunset Boulevard, recognising some street names that I have seen in movies. I also see a road sign pointing the way towards Beverly Hills. Knowing this as being the postcode area for the film and music industry's elite, I decide it must be worth a look.

I park the car and walk around the neighbourhood. Some houses are huge, hidden behind large walls, with private guards patrolling the area; whilst others are much smaller, in petite cul-de-sacs. No doubt these smaller ones are the properties that people buy just to *say* they live in Beverly Hills.

One of the small properties, on sale with a price tag of a million dollars, is offering open-house viewings, so I walk up and have a look around, speaking into a dictaphone whilst describing the property.

Not bad, I conclude, but not my first choice. There is a bar, a small lounge, an average sized kitchen, a cellar (which is a maid's quarter), and a swimming pool squeezed into a shaded back garden, traversing almost wall to wall with just enough room on one side for a couple of sun loungers (very similar in feel to the seating arrangement in the police cell).

"No thank you, it's not for me," I say to the Real Estate agent as I leave the property.

The next stop is the sign. I locate the road that I need to drive up, noticing a small convent called The Sisters of St.Clare set back behind a tall, wrought iron fence. Ironic, my surname is

117

St.Clair, so I reassure myself that I can always become a convent nun and live a life of obscurity if need be. Either this or I will throw myself off the Hollywood sign in a desperate attempt to make a statement. These random thoughts cause me to laugh at the drama queen within, recognising it as being nothing more than a brief moment of apprehension and an attempt by my ego to create its own chaos.

I drive up a narrow, long, winding road. Houses (compact but very homely) line the road, and foliage in different shades of green hangs over walls. Because of the time of day, a fresh smell of nature wafts into the car, giving my senses the impression that I am on a hillside somewhere in the Mediterranean. It feels like I am in familiar territory even though I have never been here before.

The Hollywood sign looms, growing bigger on its foundations the closer I edge to it. I take the car as far as I can but am disappointed to discover that I cannot actually get next to the sign. The large white letters are positioned over a stretch of rough terrain where people are prohibited. For some reason, I assumed that I could actually sit underneath the letters, but this is not so.

Standing in the vicinity of this global icon and knowing that I am not going to get any nearer to it, I return to the car. Impressed more with the drive than the reality of the landmark, I venture back down the road.

On the way I take my time to stop at a few different viewing spots, admiring the contemporary glass-built houses etched into the vast Hollywood hillside, each one offering the perfect retreat.

My imagination brings forth the idea of romance, showing me how nice it would be to share this moment with someone, our arms wrapped around each other as we look out at the surrounding scenery. It then gives me an insight into how enchanting it would be to share this romantic moment with someone whilst relaxing on the balcony of *that* house over there. I easily visualise us lying side-by side on cushioned sun loungers, sipping iced fruit cocktails whilst gently caressing each other's fingertips as we soak up the sun, both fully relaxed and enjoying the paradise we are blessed to be in.

I CHECK IN for one night's stay in a motel located just off Sunset Strip. It is noisy but clean. There is a double bed, a dodgy shower, and a toilet in the room, adequately meeting my immediate needs.

When I am comfortable I plug-in my computer and write an account of my day, the opening line being:

If I have this moment firmly in my grasp,
then I have the future securely in my palm.

When I finish writing, a strong sense of wanting somebody to talk to comes over me, but I refuse to give in to it. I have taken this trip because I was urged to do so. It is a conscious choice that I have made, and therefore I shall be courageous. I will not dwell on loneliness because this itself is an illusion. How can I feel lonely after hearing the world's celebratory cheers of happiness?

It is evening time, so I leave the room to go and buy some food. As I approach the entrance to the motel car park, I see a group of homeless drunk people, some with shopping trolleys filled to the brim with belongings. Upon seeing them, I decide to turn back and make do with sleep.

Waking at the crack of dawn again, I write and shower and, at the earliest possible moment, check out of the motel, driving in the direction of the beach. I find a café on the seafront, just one of a few open at this time in the morning, where I order breakfast. In no rush to go anywhere, I take my time, maybe an hour and a half, followed by a leisurely walk along the promenade.

The area is Santa Monica. It reminds me very much of Brighton. Sleeping bags move on cardboard boxes, some of them surrounded by friends already consuming their first sips of alcohol. Elderly ladies jog the length of the promenade wearing sun visors and heart rate monitors. Mothers push big-wheeled prams as they power walk and power talk. And surfers catch the early morning waves of a new day.

As I walk I notice a motel with a swimming pool in its front garden. There is parking too, so I go and book a room, having just one hour to wait until I can occupy it. The time passes quickly, and I soon settle into my next 24-hours of accommodation.

After a couple of hours of sleep, I decide to go back to Beverly Hills. Houses have always fascinated me. I see them as being more than just somewhere to live: they are an expression of self.

During my childhood, I would choose to walk specific routes, deliberately taking me past some of my favourite properties and, if nobody were around, I would peek in through cracks in a gate or climb a wall just to see what (or who) was on the other side.

As I grew older, this looking *in* turned into a fascination with wanting to see *behind the hype* of a situation, which is no doubt why Beautiful Truth lifted her veil and revealed her beauty to me. Perhaps my vision was already somewhat trained at looking *beyond* the physical appearance of something and therefore, when I was *ready to see*, the ego charade was made visible for what it really is: an illusion.....one based upon assumption with varying levels of superiority (and therefore inferiority).

I remember a fabulous house that I used to travel past on a bus. It had a magnificent frontage, one that resembled a huge art deco statue. As I passed this house I would envision the people whom lived there: a happy family, plenty of cash to go around, all openly encouraging and supporting each other in their comfortable lifestyle – you know, a very blessed group. A few years later I actually became friends with the man whom owned this property, and surprisingly his life was, for want of a better word, a mess.

He had rapidly built a successful business but was now living financially beyond his means. To compensate for his feelings of failure, due to the pressure of maintaining an outward appearance of wealth and a lifestyle he could no longer afford, he turned to alcohol - excessive amounts on a daily basis – the effect of which caused disappointment between him and his family (two beautiful children and a wife he had married pre-business days).

This friend had numerous affairs with younger women that caused even further problems in his marriage, until one day it all came crashing down. On the verge of bankruptcy he torched his business, and was buried less than two years later from the effects of liver cancer. The disease riddled his body so much that he couldn't even hold his own faeces in, becoming like a baby who needed care and attention just to go about his daily activities.

On Rodeo Drive I expect to see more people, like in the movies, but it is very quiet. The only things I see are designer shops displaying items of clothing and bling accessories, plus the odd pot-bellied tourist in knee length shorts trying to look in every direction at once. Other than this there is nothing!

No bright shopping bags being carried by desperate housewives; no poodles trotting along in stilettos; and no paparazzi chasing look-a-like celebrities. Nothing. Absolutely nothing! It's lifeless in fact, like an empty beer fridge.

I recognise more street names in the area around Rodeo Drive, so I walk down them, simply looking at the presentation around me. Several of the streets are residential, consisting mainly of box shaped, detached houses with manicured rectangular lawns at the front, the grassed area being a virtual extension of the public pavement and therefore accessible to all. Who would want to pay top dollar for this lack of privacy?

On one of the lawns there is a port-a-loo, so I make use of the convenience it presents. As I exit the cubicle, a man stood near the front door of the house smiles at me. He has a friendly face so I smile back, and then we engage in small talk. He is a builder, in charge of the house's renovation project. I ask his permission to see inside the property, enquiring about the price as he leads me through a double fronted doorway.

He gives me a full tour. There are power showers with in-built massagers, gold plated taps, walk through wardrobes, and bathrooms linking rooms. There is a bar, and a marble tiled hallway, the colours of which I like.

But overall the house isn't too impressive. It's tasteless with little creative input, making me assume that the owner doesn't really know how to effectively use four million dollars whilst confirming to me that money doesn't automatically bestow artistic discrimination. I do not tell the builder this though. I just say *thanks* and *goodbye*.

I return to the car and drive through the streets for a while, eventually parking near Beverly Garden Park where I take a short stroll. Expectation runs through my blood, although expectation of what I do not know. Do I want to see rich people, famous people, poor people or no people? Or do I just want to be here, taking in the surroundings?

In reality I don't quite know what I want, and so I walk around the neighbourhood looking at houses and peeking through gates. The question of *would I want to live here* comes to mind, my answer being an easy 'No, I wouldn't. It is too sterile for me. I like life!'

Beverley Hills looks good on TV where its image can be touched up and presented in full drag, but as for it being a community of made men, I can only ask, *Men made in what way and to whose exacting standards?*

With a pen and notebook in hand, I go into a small pizza café and sit by the window, writing down my observations and thoughts. As I sit there, a young woman with a camera stops outside and takes a photo of me.

the
therefore no
for morrow
Take
thought

Therefore
take no
thought for
the morrow

For the morrow
shall take thought,

thought the of
things take for
morrow shall For
itself

For the things of itself

I AM driving along the main coastal road towards San Francisco. When I woke this morning I wasn't too sure what to do, and this seemed like a good option. The road has already taken me past Malibu Beach, where I stopped at a convenience store and drank a coffee, watching people come and go as I checked my location on the map. Further down, at the far end of Malibu Beach, I stopped at a beachside restaurant. It was in a lovely cove surrounded by imposing cliff faces, and again I simply watched people. However, since I set off, I have a sense that something is going to happen, but I do not know what.

Sometimes feelings of uncertainty creep up, but I reassure myself that Beautiful Truth has brought me here and is seeking her own expression in my life. When I remind myself of this, I feel secure.

So far, having been in the States for three days, I have spent my time alone without much conversation. In this time I have done lots of writing and I genuinely feel that I am learning. When the only person to converse with is yourself, perception opens up many new avenues of exploration, and I have come to understand over these past few days that I am learning about *Surrender* – that of giving myself completely over to Beautiful Truth without any interference on my part (that part being my preconceived notions of how things are *supposed* to be, as dictated by external circumstances and opinions).

Because I have never lived this way before, I am enjoying it. For the first time I have total trust that everything will be good. Knowing that Beautiful Truth has *her* very best interests at heart, I am conscious that whatever happens or comes into my life each day is an essential part of her intricate plan, even if it doesn't initially make sense to me. All I have to do is to be willing to be led by her without question or uncertainty, and this is where the notion of *complete surrender* comes in.

When a person says *Do with me what you will*, they have to be willing to go the whole distance and be there until the end, like Sarah was in Amsterdam. No judging, no freaking out, just being in it for the long haul, even if it doesn't make immediate sense.

It has been almost two hours since I left Los Angeles and I am now leaving houses behind as I venture onto open road with just dirt hills on either side. It is an easy drive along a straight and uncluttered road, the sort of journey that lulls you into a relaxed state.

As I come to a junction, I notice a negative feeling engulf me from head to toe, causing my body to violently shake. It is not a minor shake: it is an all over body convulsion, to the extent that my hands turn white and my eyesight becomes blurred. This is *real* fear. It is different to the niggling voice of doubt that likes to get its two pence worth in. What I am experiencing is almost uncontrollable - my insides are frightened and my wrists are trembling as they grip the steering wheel - and I know, for my own safety, that I must stop the car.

Then the authoritative voice, the one I heard in broad daylight on my way to work, speaks to me again, just as loud and as clear as before. It doesn't happen much but when it does, I know it. I recognise this voice for who it is.

This time, in a commanding tone one would not argue with, the orders to me are, *"Turn back. You are not to leave Los Angeles. Go back, now!"*

I continue to shake until the road opens up enough for me to make a U-turn. When the car is facing back towards Los Angeles, my body calms down and peace returns, then I ask, "What do you want me to do now and where am I to go?"

I hear nothing more, however an image of the pizza café I went to the day before comes clearly to mind, so I make this my destination.

THE CAFÉ is empty except for two waitresses who are sitting together at a table chatting. They welcome me and bring a coffee. I pick up some flyers and free literature from a shelf. Quite a few advertise music events in Venice Beach and Hollywood, so I check their location against my map. Because of what I have seen in Hollywood, I don't have an inclination to stay there, making the beach area seem a better option. I also decide that the best thing I can do is stay in a traveller hostel where I may easily interact and socialise with others.

In L.A. there are several hostels to choose from, situated in different areas of the city. I ask the waitresses where they would recommend, and they give me their advice, suggesting Venice Beach because of its diversity and magnet for travellers. They point to the recommended area on the map, and I realise it is the same location which the man circled as we chatted in the jacuzzi.

I pay for my coffee and leave, knowing that I am heading for the beach to a hostel situated on a corner.

When I see the building, I am taken aback, because it is the bright, colourful building that stood out to me on my first day whilst I was driving. There is a lesson in this, showing me that

I must *trust my feelings to an even greater extent* than what I am already doing.

⸝   I remember my reaction when I first saw this building. I found it very appealing, my thoughts being, *that's cool! I should come back and check this area out.* Perhaps I should have stopped the car and checked it out there and then, rather than adding this task to a long list of *should-do's* and *do-it-laters.*

Excitement grows inside, confirmation that *this is where I am meant to be.* This is how Beautiful Truth speaks to me, via *feeling.* It is her way of communicating the way – the path – to the unfolding (the execution) of her perfect plan.

Sometimes the feelings I experience are subtle, like a gentle whisper; and other times they are pronounced, like a shout or a cheer. My duty is to *discern her words* and then respond whilst not confusing her dialogue or dialect with that of the ego. *Careful observation* is key to understanding her language, something that becomes much easier the more I listen and respond to her directions.

On the remarkable day in Amsterdam I went along with what felt right, and it was the most amazing day of my life. At other times I have gone with what I felt I *ought* to do (even if it has not felt right), and there has always been some sort of consequence to pay.

It is easy to use the excuse that there is always a consequence, but this is another myth perpetrated by the ego and its many players. There are *results,* and there are *consequences.* Results occur from being *in harmony* with the meticulous plan of Beautiful Truth, denoting positive outcomes because of one's alignment with Truth and therefore fuelling a smooth transition to life's next essential event upon the path of Beautiful Truth.

Consequences, on the other hand, denote the outcome of a judgement made in error, that is, of an erroneous way of thinking. When one's decision-making process is flawed, a consequence will be paid because it does not benefit the whole. The ego cannot reason from this viewpoint (i.e. of the whole), and therefore its ways always lead to consequences that require some form of correction.

Who, when she had found
one pearl of great price

all
and
sold
bought
had that Went
she it

Went and sold all that she had
and
bought
it

THE RECEPTIONIST at the hostel shows me a private room. It is perfect: double bed, bathroom, TV, fridge, sofa, and two large windows, with one of them opening up to give an unobstructed view of the sea. There is a table positioned in front of this window, making it an ideal location from which to write. Without hesitation I pay up front for one week's stay.

After settling in I walk to the beach, unaware of the place to which I have been brought. As I turn on to the boardwalk I am totally blown away. It is like a full-on carnival: performers, art & craft stalls, cafés, skate boarders and roller skaters moving to music, as well as many more colourful sights and sounds, all set against the backdrop of a beautiful white sandy beach that is being tenderly stroked by the Californian sea breeze.

If someone had presented me with a catalogue to the world, along with an opportunity of selecting my ideal location from it, I could not have chosen a more perfect place in which to absorb myself. Never in a million years did I think that a place such as this existed. It is like taking all the elements that I love about life and then fitting them together into one fantastic whole, meaning that I get to enjoy it all without much effort on my part.

Venice Beach is a location that has *every aspect of me* in it, as though my Beautiful Truth has painted this perfect atmosphere ahead of my arrival, preparing a place for me that she knows I will love.

And I do love it. It's fantastic.

This area is also home to the legend of Jim Morrison. His large and imposing image is painted on the side of a building that overlooks the beach, giving him a front row seat from which to observe the goings on of others who mimic his footsteps.

I recall a film about his life, where he falls in love and reads poetry to his girl, playfully chasing her around the palm trees that stand to attention along this very boardwalk. I imagine myself doing the same, running and laughing from one intimate moment to the next.

It's a romantic notion, I know, but I enjoy it.

I HAVE now been here for three full days, but the ease with which I have settled in makes it seem like I am a veteran of the place.

Each day I take an early morning walk along the boardwalk, a narrow stretch of pavement that runs parallel to the beach. There are basket ball hoops, skate areas, palm readers, lifeguard stations, shops, cafés, bars, stilt walkers – the list is varied and endless, and is a continual feast on the senses.

Yesterday I went to a drum circle where people bang anything and everything, the combined outcome being a tribal song that falls in tune with the beating of the heart. If there is nothing to bang, then people dance in the centre of the circle, saluting the sun on their hands and knees as it descends on the day.

The sound of the instruments, from conga drums and bongos, to rattles and tambourines, has a meditative effect on the mind. It is an audio vibe that ties everyone together, because when one person starts to change their tempo, others follow suit. If the beat speeds up, all the percussive effects speed up. And if it slows down, the same chain reaction occurs.

The room is proving perfect too. It is filled with sunshine every day, and the smell of the sea is the first impression my nose receives on waking. Wine is also very reasonable, retailing at a few dollars for one litre of renowned quality. California is a grape growers haven and is one of the most popular wine regions in the world.

It literally feels as though I have found my heaven on earth, and I can easily see myself spending the rest of my days here. So I write about this place, all the while consumed with a romantic notion of love and endless vacations.

Today is the fourth day. I am chilling in my room, effortlessly listening to a conversation that is taking place on the balcony below. The room phone rings. It is Pat, a traveller from England whom I met on the second day. She is also staying in the hostel, in a shared dormitory on a lower floor. Her girlfriend - her lover - arrived in Los Angeles this afternoon and she wants me to come to the communal lounge to meet her.

About twenty minutes later I go down to the lounge and make some introductions, after which I walk over to the stereo to put a CD on. A young man (he looks early twenties) sits on a sofa nearest the stereo and so, out of courtesy, I ask if it would bother him if I were to put some music on.

His smile is huge – cheek-to-cheek – and his long hair is in two Native American-style braids. The music won't bother him, he informs me, still smiling.

I go and sit with Pat and her girlfriend. She asks to borrow eighty dollars so that she can hire a car. Pat says she will return the money to me in a few days, her reason for the loan being that she is just waiting for her mum to transfer the cash from England. As a safety measure she says that I can keep her passport.

We walk to the cash machine and I withdraw the money, after which the three of us return to the hostel lounge where we chat. I notice that the young man has now moved to the opposite side of the room, where he sits watching TV. As the three of us talk, he interrupts with the random question, "Do you like The Simpsons?"

Pat and her girlfriend do. I don't watch it, and so think nothing of telling him this. He is silent for a few minutes but then starts to berate me, the reason being that he is stupefied a person of the modern world doesn't actually watch The Simpsons. It is something he cannot comprehend, so much so that he feels the need to make continual sarcastic digs at me, causing me to become irritated.

I find his comments unnecessary and out of context, wondering why he is sweating over such a trivial matter and feeling quite certain that I would have received more politeness and respect from him if I had told him that I was about to detonate a bomb. But I do not tell him this, preferring to ignore him whilst questioning within: *who* exactly *does he think he is?*

The Simpsons finishes and the young man heads over to where we are sitting. Pat and her girlfriend are getting ready to leave for the evening, so they show that they are not too fussed about conversing with him. He turns his attention to me and, before he can say anything, I demand, "So, what are you about then?" (my underlying, finger-pointing question being, What makes *you* so special?).

Ready for an arrogant answer, I am both surprised and pleased when he says, "Oh, I am one of those crazy people who believe they are going to change the world. The difference is...... I am going to do it!"

The ice is broken and my temporary barrier melts. "Cool," I reply. "I am one of those people too. How do you intend to do it?"

Looking equally surprised and pleased at my response, he replies, "Through my music. What about you?"

"Through my writing," I say.

A cheeky smile comes to his face, so I decide to put him on the spot. "Go on then, sing!" I command.

Inwardly I feel smug, assuming that he will feel too embarrassed to break out into song. But, to my complete surprise, he doesn't. He simply sits down and sings, not caring who is around or who is listening.

"Every player's got a purpose,
everybody's on the team,
everybody's got places that they're
heading to,
and all the places they've been."

As he sings, I notice that there is a genuine sweetness and sincerity in his demeanour. Respectfully and somewhat intrigued, I continue listening.

"Everybody's got a vision,
everybody's got a dream,
sometimes you're blinded by the
false gods of the flesh,
so that it's so hard to see."

His song is called **Ecosystem.**

When he has finished singing, he asks, "What are you three doing this evening?"

"They are going out," I reply, gesturing towards Pat and her friend, "but I don't have any plans."

"Do you want to hang out with me?"

His name is Daniel, and twenty minutes later we are walking along the boardwalk with a quart bottle of Vodka each in our pockets. It is evening time and there is a different atmosphere in the air. As we are walking, Daniel moves me to his left side (furthest away from the shops) in a protective manner.

"You should be careful along here at night," he warns, "it is quite dangerous. You see those people over there?"

I look in the same direction as him and see a group of youths hanging around a fast food booth.

"They are a bit trigger happy," he continues. "Those young lads come down here carrying guns, sometimes using them just to prove how tough they are. If you can avoid this area at night, then do so."

Daniel tells me more about himself, things like how he moved to California from Chicago, as well as some of the stuff he has done in L.A. with his music. He talks easily of his *life's vision* and the effect he sees his music having on the world.

We sit on the beach on a small group of rocks. The sea is close to us, and I sense it playing a game of musical statues each time my back is turned. We laugh a lot and talk a lot, all the while looking out at the panoramic view of Venice Beach.

I can tell from talking to him that I am going to like him. Our upbringings are different, literally at opposite ends of the scale, and yet we have connected. Even though he looks young, there is an old wise head on his shoulders. He has lived in gangland neighbourhoods in inner city Chicago, and he understands the ways of the streets in places like L.A. He tells me of a few situations he has witnessed, along with the safety checks he always makes when in certain areas of the city.

"But I am not afraid," he says, confidently. "I have God with me, and wherever I am, there He is, protecting me. I wouldn't be in this situation, here in Los Angeles, if it weren't part of the mission. God doesn't waste anything. I know that everything I experience is in preparation for greater things."

As he talks of God, I think of Beautiful Truth, realising that we are referring to the same magnificent entity. I like what I am hearing.

When the vodka is finished, we decide to go to a bar. Daniel has a place in mind, *somewhere*, he says, *where we can really laugh*. As we are walking to the bar he stops and breaks two long twigs off a large bush, which he then passes to me. "Here, thread them through my braids," he instructs. "I am going to make my hair stand out horizontally at the sides."

I fiddle with the twigs, pushing and twisting them through his tight braids, the result being one of the funniest hairstyles I have ever seen. Passers-by also find it hilarious, with random shouts of *Pippi (*Longstocking*)* grabbing our attention.

In America the legal drinking age is twenty-one, and all venues request to see official identification of everyone who enters. Upon arrival at the bar, a doorman checks Daniel's driving license and then asks to see my identification. Knowing that I don't have any on me, I instinctively open my jacket to reveal my bulging breasts in a tight T-Shirt.

"Here, this is my I.D." I say to the doorman, walking confidently past him and into the bar.

When we get inside Daniel high fives me and congratulates me on the genius move; and together we laugh at the doorman's speechless expression when faced with my voluptuous chest and no-nonsense attitude.

We put our arms around each other as we walk back to the hostel, arranging to meet the next day in the café across the road. He doesn't stay in the hostel: he just visits daily to watch The Simpsons, something the owner permits him to do because he used to work there in exchange for a bed.

.

153

IT IS eleven a.m. and I am sitting in the café in front of a computer, surfing on the Internet. Daniel arrives and gives me a friendly hug. He wears a denim jacket, nice fitting jeans, plus his trademark braids. His T-shirt fits perfectly on his body, and he has the style that I like: retro yet individual; modern with a vintage twist.

However, the physical - the external - is not what this is about. I am interested in the *inner* him, for I feel there is something very special there. Last night we had a great time, and as we both relaxed I saw his very own Beautiful Truth peeking through his thin veil, introducing me to a lovely man waiting patiently in the wings of his stage.

We order coffee and chat, and he tells me more about his music. He is clearly passionate and enthusiastic about life and the work before him, elements which I find to be rare in people of all ages. When I question what his back-up plan is should his music vision not work out, he replies that he doesn't have one. There is no plan B, only a plan A.

"Anyone who has a plan B is accepting failure before they have even started," he says. "If you are confident in what you are doing and you understand the reasons why you are doing it, then only a plan A is needed. Just ensure that you give that one plan your all. Having a back-up plan is nothing more than telling yourself that plan A isn't likely to work, a subtle belief that will cause Plan A to fail. I don't play that game."

I love his reasoning. It makes so much sense, and yet I have never heard anyone say this before. He then points out that God doesn't need a plan B, it is only people who do, something which Daniel attributes to a lack of faith (within the individual) in the Creator and His Intelligent design. I tell Daniel that I fully understand what he is saying, because this is the same conclusion that I have come to regarding the ways of Beautiful Truth - the *great unseen power within an individual that knows exactly what she is doing and why she is doing it*, something that we, as individuals, may never fully comprehend.

He asks me to tell him more about my trip to Los Angeles, and so I talk about the build up of events that led me to getting on the plane.

I explain about my unfolding journey, and how I am observing it so as to fully understand how the power within me works so that I may teach others about her.

"It is a passion that consumes me," I tell him, "so much so that I have turned my back on my life.......as in my career, my home, everything that was *me*. I don't know where it

155

will lead or what I will be doing. I just know that I am meant to do this."

This excites him, and he tells me that I remind him of Amelia Earhart and Joan of Arc, two of his female inspirations. I feel myself blush at this lovely, unique compliment.

Daniel shares his passion for the Bible with me - a book he has read in great depth and one that he continually makes reference to. He takes a copy out of his bag and I notice that it is well read: tattered along the edges of the pages. He knows quotes and passages by heart, along with where they can be found in the book. I find this somewhat intriguing, and so decide to open up about the experiences I have encountered with Jesus Christ. As well as telling Daniel about the voice that I heard several times, I explain how the Bible and Christ has always been alien to me, mainly because of the stigma surrounding them but also because I am not even certain whether the stories in the Bible are real.

"Let's put everything aside," Daniel says confidently, "as to whether the stories in this book are real or not. Get that out of your head or, better still, if it will make you feel comfortable, let's assume that the stories in the Bible are made up. Now let's look at the teachings of Jesus." He opens the book, "This small section......these few pages.....are Jesus' teachings. If you were to actually read them, you will find no fault in his message whatsoever. I have tried to give weight to the arguments that Jesus is a myth, but my conclusion is that it really doesn't matter whether he is or he isn't. It is about his teachings and what they mean, and nobody can deny that these are great lessons. Also, if Jesus is a myth, the fact remains that somebody had to write them – to conceive them – and therefore they possessed the understanding contained within these lessons. What more needs to be said? The argument falls flat on its face because it is really irrelevant."

"That's a very good point," I reply. "I have never thought about it like that before."

"No, a lot of people don't. They are too busy arguing about whether he is real, whether he is God, whether he is the messiah, all that stuff, as if this is more important than what he actually said. It is not the teachings of Jesus that are misleading. It is people misunderstanding and misinterpreting them. Whether the Bible is real or not," says Daniel, holding the tattered book in his hand, "the stories and parables within it all contain deeper meanings that provide a wonderful foundation for life. If ever I have a problem, I just open a page and the solution is given to me."

We order another drink and continue our conversation of the Bible, with Daniel stating that if I was to read the book in its physical context only, then it is unlikely to make much sense to me. However, by seeking to understand the *metaphysical* aspect of the text, I will find an entire approach to spiritual awareness that is as relevant today as it was when it was first written.

When he explains it like this, it seems as though reading the Bible in its physical context only is just the same as applying the ego's perspective when seeking to navigate life, in that it is shallow, misleading, and self serving.

"My goal is to take the message of Truth to people in the simplest way possible" he says, "and music is the most accessible product in the world. It is a *universal tool for good*. I intend to use it to infiltrate the illusion and then pull it all down from within. I want to see peace and happiness engulf our planet. Could you imagine what the world would be like if it all came crashing down......if the illusion of life could no longer sustain itself?"

As he speaks I lose myself in his words and my heart beats fast, as though it is excited and could burst through my lungs at any moment. Daniel speaks my language but so much more definitively. He is certain about what he has to do in his lifetime – he has a *clear purpose* – and it makes me feel *alive*, with a longing to spend as much time as possible in his company.

His *enthusiasm for life*, coupled with an *awareness of his infinite potential* in it, is infectious, like nothing I have ever encountered before. There are aspects of the ego-driven personality that I see in him, for example a boyish arrogance at times, but this is a trait that will not last because of his whole approach to life.

He openly talks about and envisions a *spiritual revolution of the heart*, one in which love abounds for people and life everywhere. His terminology empowers and uplifts, and it fascinates me. I am certain that this is the same revolution as taught by Jesus Christ.

The fact that Daniel sleeps on the street doesn't bother me. He is the first homeless person I have met, and I am surprised at his level of cleanliness. I naively assumed that all homeless people were like the shopping trolley drunks in Hollywood, but this is obviously not the case, giving me another wonderful lesson of why I must not judge others based on their physical appearance alone.

Daniel's homelessness is a personal choice. Because of the cost of accommodation in

Los Angeles, he made the conscious decision to live on the streets so that he could focus on his music. At present he works nights in a fast food take-away, his goal being to save up for a camper van. This also enables him to perform during the daytime on Venice Beach boardwalk and Santa Monica promenade – the city's hotbeds for tourists and performers.

He has some good friends, one of whom gives him the keys to his VW at nights, meaning that Daniel gets to sleep on a pull down bed in an enclosed shelter if he is not working his night-shift. If the van is not available, he knows of some safe places to sleep along the beach, like underneath the various sets of wooden steps. There are public showers where he cleans himself, and sometimes he travels to the YMCA for a hot shower and decent wash. He admits that at times he finds it tough, but when this happens he writes a song, or sings, or listens to music.

Knowing that a person's art is an expression of their inner self, I ask Daniel if I can read his lyrics. As a writer I fully understand that the real person, the one lurking in the deeper recesses of the closet, cannot hide behind a pen because the real person is the ink in the pen. I believe that if I see his lyrics, then I will view his Beautiful Truth in full.

We are sat on the beach and I have a folder in my hands. It is Daniel's collection of songs. He sits next to me with his guitar. I press record on a dictaphone and, starting at the first page, he explains the story behind the song and then he sings it.

As we go through the lyrics, I am taken aback at the depth and insight of the young man at my side. Never before have I felt such a thrill at being in the company of one person, and surprisingly, I start thinking about how I would love to spend every day with him - waking up, talking, laughing, being together - just hanging out like the best of friends and enjoying life as it unfolds.

Daniel requests to see my writing, so we return to the hostel to collect my laptop. We go to a small apartment that belongs to his friend where I show him the book I am working on. He reads the first couple of pages and then, unexpectedly, jumps up and throws his arms around me.

The full force of his body causes me to fall back. Genuinely thrilled, he informs me that many girls have told him that they share his vision for life but, when it came to the substance of it, they didn't. He clearly sees that I do!

It seems my writing has the same effect on him that his lyrics have on me.

Blessed is she
who hungers and thirsts after righteousness

righteousness

and
is who after Blessed
thirsts hungers
she

shall

For
be

she

satisfied

For she
shall be
satisfied

DANIEL IS very sociable and knows many people in the vicinity of Venice Beach. He engages in light-hearted conversation with a wide variety of individuals, and whenever he does so he effortlessly introduces me to them. This openness feels nice, as though he is inviting me more and more into his personal life. I find his approach warm and inclusive, something which I like..... a lot.

He regularly stops and chats to Mongwau, a Native American who occupies a stall selling traditional goods to tourists; and who also provides wisdom and spiritual advice to the seekers-of-something-more. Mongwau lives at the beach in a camper van, sharing its compact interior with his small dog, the relationship of which reminds me more of man and wife than it does man and animal. This is not so strange though. People of all ages are more devoted to their pets than they are other humans, the prime reason being the unconditional love displayed by animals for their devoted keeper.

Another person Daniel routinely greets is a roller-blading guitar player who dresses like a Sikh, his long dreads wrapped in a foot high turban and his body covered in several layers of white cotton. This man always acknowledges with a smile but rarely stops for conversation, halting for photographs when people ask whilst charging them a fee for the privilege. Apparently he lives in an affluent area of L.A. and, even though he looks like he is just hanging out and doing nothing but skating and smiling, he is in fact working the boardwalk and generating a substantial income.

"The boardwalk might look like a laidback place to be," Daniel tells me, "but it is quite ruthless underneath the facade. People here are in competition to make money from tourists, with the regular vendors being very territorial about where they place their stalls to conduct business. Don't be fooled by appearances. Some of those trading themselves as the most spiritual here," he continues, pointing towards a palm reader, "can behave like some of the most unspiritual people you could ever meet. Remember, spirituality often takes the form of nothing more than a consumer product or fashion statement to lots of people, and traders know this."

Like many other major cities, Los Angeles is fashion conscious, a place where weird, wonderful, tasteful and tasteless dress senses parade freely on the public catwalk. The manner in which people clothe themselves in Venice Beach reminds me more of the way people dress when attending music festivals, making my eclectic wardrobe the perfect accompaniment for this environment.

Daniel and I share our passion for vintage clothing by mooching in and out of second hand shops, where we try on hats, jackets, T-shirts, and other items. He takes me to some off-the-beat places where I discover several classic items of clothing, one of them being a figure-hugging retro-style denim dress. It fits perfectly, and he compliments me on how sexy I look in it.

In-between our adventures we talk about our philosophies and experiences, and I share with him my method of *seeking to understand more* about Beautiful Truth by drawing analogies to every day activities. Our clothes shopping experience has given me much food for thought, and I tell Daniel how I can relate the ego to a person's wardrobe.

Some people never get rid of clothes that no longer serve a purpose to them, as though they are frightened of *letting-go*.

Others are so attached to certain items of clothing that without them they feel lost. And this is the same for the ego, for the way that people have dressed their personality in habits, beliefs, and illusionary expectations of life that don't actually suit who they truly are on the inside.

Removing the veil is literally about *stripping away the ego* until just the naked and Beautiful Truth is left standing. When this is done, a person is then able to *clothe their life* in the Ideal contained *within* them.

As I talk to Daniel, I notice his eyes soften, as though he is fascinated by my words. When I have finished speaking, he hugs me and says, "I love it when you speak like this. Anyone who can bind spirituality and nakedness is my sort of woman!"

His comment makes me laugh, and it feels great knowing that he enjoys a tongue-in-cheek take on life just as much as I do.

IN OUR five days together we have done much talking, and I know that I have never met anybody like him before. He has a deep faith in God that I find admirable, a complete trust that, at every moment, he is cared for and nurtured by a presence that functions on a much deeper level.

Daniel fully believes that every single situation that comes into or leaves his life is an essential part of God's plan. He has many real-life stories to back up his beliefs, proving more and more to him that there can be no other way in life but to heed the inner voice: the intimate language of God (or, as I understand it, the whispers of Beautiful Truth).

Before he arrived in Los Angeles he had spent fourteen months in San Diego, another Californian city along the coast with a much more chilled way of life. During this time he regularly sang outside bars or on the beach, with passers-by and friends sometimes giving him loose change. When money allowed, he would pay for a bed in a beachfront hostel, an abode that housed long-term, fun-loving beach bums, and an environment Daniel enjoyed being in.

On one particular day though Daniel had no money, and unless he came up with the cost of the bed he would be required to leave the hostel and sleep rough. However, this could not be an option for him due to the fact that the night before he had been beaten up, innocently suffering the aftermath of a young lady's loose mouth. Daniel was tired and bruised, and he felt a longing to sleep in a comfortable place so as to recover and replenish his energy.

Going out to sing on the street was the last thing he needed, but it was something that had to be done to if he was to retain his bed. Before he left the hostel with his guitar, Daniel said a heartfelt prayer to God, asking Him to make it easy to secure enough money for a bed for the night. With his guitar in hand Daniel went out and started singing, fully expecting that his prayers would be answered. They were. The first person that walked past dropped the amount of money he needed into his guitar case, giving him a surplus of only 50 cents but enough with which to return to the hostel for the night.

This is just one of his many stories, the common theme in them being about *his genuine prayers always being answered,* and why he knows that there are *no mistakes in his life*.

He admits that Los Angeles is proving psychologically challenging compared to San Diego, but he also believes it is a place where he *needs to be at this moment in time*. Daniel knows that God has a plan for his life, with his time in

L.A. being but one piece in the jigsaw. He perceives it all as being God's genius handiwork, a fact that is further confirmed by our recent meeting, as though our coming together is a union that was conceived long before we ever physically met.

Daniel tells me that a couple of days before our first meeting, he had sat on the beach and had a conversation with God. Whilst speaking to Him he saw, with clarity, the spiritual make-up of his ideal woman, something that has never happened before. During this conversation, Daniel had a full realisation of the *inner qualities* of the woman with whom he wanted to share his life. He talked about her attitude, her personality, and her love of life; he emphasised his female role models and how his ideal woman would possess their qualities of strength, courage, love, determination, and intelligence.

But more than anything, it was about her understanding and sharing his vision for life; and about her fully supporting him in his life's work.

He admits that initially he wasn't attracted to me, because even though I looked sexy I gave the appearance of being a stuck-up professional, someone who was very head strong and spent more time in a boardroom than at the beach. However, now that he has gotten to know me, he believes me to be the most amazing woman he has ever met, with me naturally fulfilling all of the ideals he had spoken to God about just a few days earlier.

I agree with Daniel, telling him that I feel exactly the same. My first impressions of him weren't the greatest. I judged him as being arrogant and rather too immature for me. However, as I have got to know him, I believe he is my ideal man: the perfect partner and playmate, someone who I could spend every moment of every day with. He intrigues and fascinates me, he inspires and strengthens me, he teaches and yet learns from me, and on top of all this, he makes me laugh.

During our conversation, Daniel takes my hands and looks directly into my eyes. "You know we're going to get married, don't you?"

Immediately my voice replies, "Yes, I do."

Since our second day together the thoughts of him developing into a very fine and genuine man have gone through my mind. I had even concluded that someone, somewhere, would spend the rest of their life with him and would therefore be the most fortunate woman alive. So when he tells me that he knows we are going to get married, I decide that the woman in question shall be me.

It feels a bit selfish, and I wonder if I am really the woman he sees me as, but I know in my heart that this treasure cannot pass from my hands. To give it away would be like discovering a mighty pearl at the bottom of the ocean, only to toss it aside for someone else to benefit from, someone whom doesn't appreciate its beauty like I do.

At this moment in time I cannot conceive walking away from Daniel and never seeing him again. It would be far too much of a regret in my lifetime, and I would continually look back, always wondering *what-if*. This feeling runs so deep that marrying him is the easy, risk free option. Walking away is the difficult option and is one that I am not willing to pursue.

I have heard it said time and time again that you know when you meet your marriage mate. There is a feeling that comes over you, confirming you are going to be with this person for the rest of your life. I always thought this was a myth, something people say to add a touch of romance to their union, but now I know it is true. Within a couple of days I knew that I wanted to spend the rest of my life with Daniel, even though man-made logic and public opinion would advise contrary to this.

I have always held a deep belief of there existing a great love between two people, one which traverses mountains and oceans, and one which breeds loyalty and trust like no other relationship on Earth. I have never doubted its existence, although I have assumed it was not for me because perhaps I am too wild or not innocent enough to encounter it. But many times I have felt this wonderful love, deep down in my heart. I suppose it *is fairy tale love*, where the union brings about an amazing and happy life for the lovers involved.

Some women dream of princes and fabulous dresses, and of palaces and prestige. But for me, the *ideal in my life* has been this amazing love in which trust and deep respect are in natural abundance, qualities I believe to be the harmonising and uniting factor of every living entity on our planet.

Totally unexpected, Daniel says, "If we are both certain that we want to spend our lives together, then let's get married tomorrow. I don't see the need to wait. Do you?"

Without hesitation, I say "Yes, let's do it."

With this impossible men is

With men this is impossible

God all things are possible With
possible With God, all things are possible

LATER THAT evening I decide to contact my sister to let her know my whereabouts. It is the first contact I have had with my family since leaving England. The email is short and to the point, stating that I am in L.A. and that, in a couple of days, I shall have a surprise for her and Mother. I ask her to pass on my love, followed by an instruction of *not to worry*.

We also pay a visit to Jochen, one of Daniel's good friends. When Daniel informs him that we will be getting married tomorrow, his face paints a picture of shock that makes us all laugh. Daniel tells me that Jochen reacted this way because the last time they socialised together (less than a week ago), they had joked that they were going to avoid serious relationships believing that women might prevent them each from fulfilling their potential in life. Now, just a few days after this masculine display of comradeship, here was Daniel announcing his plans to marry a stranger from England!

The response from others is varied, with several people warning Daniel to be cautious of my intentions. Each year foreigners visit the States with the sole aim of marrying a citizen so as to secure a green card, giving them permanent residency in the country. This is the first thought some people have with regards our marriage. A

British girl who is staying at the hostel congratulates me on my 'balls' of marrying (presumably for a green card), commenting that she wishes she had the guts to do it. Some other people at the hostel don't say anything, but look at me with questioning eyes.

There are a few people who genuinely share our excitement and offer us their heartfelt congratulations, with Jochen being one of them. He informs us that he is not working tomorrow and would therefore love nothing more than to be Daniel's best man.

The three of us arrive at the Los Angeles Courthouse the next day, excited and prepared for a wedding. We are informed of the protocol involved as well as office opening hours, meaning that we will have to return on another day.

The next date for official marriage ceremonies is at the dawning of the spring equinox - a *time of new birth* - on March 21st.

Where two or three are
gathered in my name

two or where name gathered in go three For my

There
them
the
There I AM
In
of
midst
in the midst of them
AM

THREE DAYS later (and nine days in total since meeting), I shower and make an effort with my presentation, wearing a white gypsy-style bustier top and a pair of pale pink flared trousers. My skin is tanned, and I have a healthy glow on my body and face. Wanting to do something special, I place a pink crystal between my eyebrows and I decorate my fingernails with a pretty stick-on design. I wear some new sandals offset by a diamanté toe ring and pretty anklet, with two fresh flowers taken from a bouquet given to me earlier (by Daniel) in my hair.

The sun is shining into the room, and Daniel plays his guitar on the balcony below. Knowing that a momentous occasion is upon us I take a walk to the beach, sitting on some rocks to write by allowing my thoughts to flow unhindered onto the paper. It feels strange but nice, and I take the opportunity to feel if there are any doubts lurking deep within. Nothing bubbles to the surface, confirmation that this is the next essential step on my life's journey.

When I have finished writing I stand up, letting the sea breeze blow over my body. I become weightless, feeling like nothing more than a block of air suspended in air, as though the breeze is passing through me but that I too am the breeze.

Some women plan their wedding day for years, idealising the dress, venue, setting, and many other aspects, literally perfecting every detail of (to them) the most important day of their lives. I have never done this because I couldn't imagine myself marrying anyone. Obviously, wearing a wedding dress is something that all girls think of at some point in their adolescence – me included – but other than this, I haven't given my wedding day any thought.

Daniel and I take a bus to a building not far from the airport, enjoying the ride and finding many opportunities to giggle. Whilst sat on the bus, the realisation dawns on me that this is in fact my perfect wedding day. No fuss, no big parade of fanciness, and no stress about whose demands (other than my own) shout the loudest. It is just my man and I, and the expression of our genuine desire to spend the rest of our lives together.

When we get off the bus we make the short walk to the register office. Talking and laughing, I look at my future husband as he leads the way. He too has made an effort with his dress, and he looks lovely. He wears a form-fitting vintage cowboy shirt and jeans, whilst his immaculate braids rest over his shoulders.

We do not have wedding rings because we have decided to have them tattooed on our fingers after the ceremony. Tattoos are permanent and unique to us, something we shall design together and wear for the rest of our lives. We have already set our minds on the design, opting for an eagle in the style of a Native American cave drawing. Its simple wings wrap around the finger, whilst its minimalistic torso represents the priceless jewel.

The eagle also holds a greater symbolic meaning for us with it being a statement of freedom, as though in marriage we have received a new set of wings with which we soar the heights together. Not only this, but Daniel's surname of *Orlick* is Polish in origin, and when translated means *eagle*. For me this is perfection and romance: the very two attributes which every bride craves on her wedding day.

Upon arrival at the L.A. Courthouse we are asked who our witnesses are. Not having any, we ask a man who is in attendance at another wedding if he will do the honour for us. Our second witness is the marriage official who is conducting the service.

Standing side-by-side with our hands tightly wrapped together, the registrar asks, "Do you, Daniel Orlick, take this woman to be your lawfully wedded wife?"

He replies, loud and confident, "Yes sir, I do!

I am asked if *I, Joanne St.Clair, take this man to be my lawfully wedded husband*, to which I reply, "Yes, I do."

And then we are pronounced,

Man and Wife.

ONE WEEK later, before the sun has cast her rays upon the new day, Daniel and I are in the hostel foyer waiting for a taxi to come and take me to the airport. Since our wedding day we have made plans for our future, the first stage being for me to return to England in order to sort out household business. Our goal is to rent out the house, and then I shall come back to the States to become Daniel's manager in the music industry. We estimate that this should take no longer than approximately eight weeks.

I tear a section off a used envelope, upon which I scribble my address and phone number. On another piece of envelope I write down the number of the hostel's public pay phone. Whilst standing in the payphone booth, I take a flyer off the noticeboard and write *Daniel Orlick Rocks My World* on the back, re-pinning it on the board as a reminder to Daniel (when he discovers it) that I am still with him even though I will be over five thousand miles away.

Once I leave the hostel, my husband will go back to living on the streets until I return from the UK. During this period we shall speak to each other at arranged times on public payphones, and also by email.

As a safety measure for visa issues, Daniel gives me his birth certificate and I have an original copy of our marriage certificate. The only other evidence of our marriage union is the tattoo on my finger and a handful of photos of our wedding ceremony.

When I see the taxi arrive, a tear comes to my eye. Daniel tells me to be strong and that soon we shall be together again. He is positive and upbeat, and even though I share the magic of our situation, heaviness hangs over me. We hug and say goodbye, and then I get into the taxi and leave, knowing that I am heading back to England to the life I left less than four weeks earlier, my trip cut much shorter than anticipated and yet my future spread before me like a red carpet.

As I am driven to the airport, I start thinking of my journey and the outcome of it. When I left for Los Angeles I had no expectations, only the goal of understanding the depths of Beautiful Truth within me and a deep yearning to observe my very own ideal and beautiful life manifest. As my trip unfolded, I listened more and more to the voice within, letting her show me through signs, conversations, and feelings, where I should go and what I should do. I made every attempt to surrender to her, refusing to interfere with her plans by seeking to do things my way i.e. by my limited understanding of life and its immediate environment.

The result has been mind blowing and exhilarating, but the thought of returning to the U.K. is scary. On the one hand everything feels different; and yet on the other hand it all feels the same. Man made reasoning - the ego - tells me that I may never see my husband again; whilst Beautiful Truth whispers that we shall be reunited soon and all will be good.

As the taxi ushers me closer to the airport, I start to relate my current situation to that of my raving days, when all night parties in random fields would bring thousands of people together from all walks of life. These gatherings were illegal but this didn't stop people from being magnetised by the music and the vibe; and from following vague directions scribbled on torn slips of paper - similar to the piece of envelope in my hand – leading them to an amazing night of dancing, acceptance, and togetherness.

I see that the directions to the greatest gathering in the world are already scribed on my heart, and they were made known to me in Amsterdam. I began to follow these directions the moment I consciously chose to heed the words of my very own Beautiful Truth, *an amazing power within in me that has a perfect plan for my life.*

.

Beautiful Truth knows what I love, and she knows what makes me abundantly happy. She knows where my life party is at, she knows how to get there, and she knows what is waiting for me at the destination.

As the taxi comes to a halt near the *Departures* entrance, I realise that I have met my eternal dancing partner. I have no idea of what is ahead of me, but I clearly hear the music and I feel the beat, knowing that Daniel and I are grooving to the same tune. This is what it is about: nothing more, nothing less.

Before entering LAX Airport, I turn and take a breath of the early morning Californian air. Wiping a tear from my eye, I say, "Goodbye Daniel Orlick, I love you."

I walk through the automatic doors towards the Departure lounge in the same contented manner in which I exited the police cell; and with the same deep knowing that an irrevocable change has taken place in my life, one which feels just as amazing as the State of Happiness declared upon the world.

Like a fanatical hijacker of the good times, my ego demands, "What will you do if things don't go to plan?"

But straight away, calm and assured, my Beautiful Truth whispers, "Just be there until the end. This is all I ask of you."

Beautiful

always

with

is

Truth

you

The

The Beautiful
Truth is with
you always

of the
the
until
world
Even
end

Even unto
the end of
the world

WHAT HAPPENED NEXT?

AS IT turned out, nothing that they expected.

Being a spouse of a USA citizen, it was required that Joanne possesses a marriage visa (an application that can take a minimum of two years to process) in order to return to her husband. Having no income, Daniel was not in a position to act as a sponsor for Joanne on this visa, and so started an era that came as a surprise to both of them.

All plans and preconceived notions of what they thought they would do together went out of the window. At times they were emotionally and mentally tried (especially when apart from each other for the majority of their first two years of marriage), but in their hearts they knew that Beautiful Truth had a very special mission planned for them, a unique role that only they could fulfill.

Both Daniel and Joanne had made a promise that they would be there until the end, irrespective of what life asked of them. To this they were, and are, committed.........

Ten years
and two
children later

years two O later and
children
Ten

And this is the special mission assigned them by Beautiful Truth:

"It is into your hands that I lovingly and willingly place this task.

I Am the force that weaves and fuels life. Those whom love me with their whole heart are the leaders and chosen messengers of my works.

Your ever burning passion for me means that you have selected yourself as the torch bearers of my secrets, and it is these secrets that I ask you to share throughout the world.

Your music, words, art, and your love for each other are the platforms of my expression. I will abundantly provide you with all that you need to fulfill this work in your lifetime, because in your union both the DJ and the Dancer have come together, just as Heaven and Earth becomes one, as do Mother and Child.

Go forth with joy, always assured that whatever happens,

I will be there until the end."

On September 14th 2012, Daniel Orlick and Joanne St.Clair launched *Naked Raver,* a company that creates and publishes music, books, and art that enhance the beauty of a woman's mind by encouraging her to believe in the magnificent presence within.

*Na*ked:*

The stripping bare of
illusionary concepts of limitation.

*Ra*ver:*

She who dances to the tune of
her own indwelling spirit,
one whose notes are love and trust.

www.thenakedraver.com

Recommended reading:

Statue in the Square, by Joanne St.Clair

Costa del Social, by Joanne St.Clair

Recommended listening:

Ocean, by Daniel Orlick

This Is Our Day, by Daniel Orlick

She's Coming Clean, by Daniel Orlick

Recommended viewing:

Awakening the Giant, by Daniel Orlick

50 Shades of Groove, by Daniel Orlick

When The Clock Strikes Peace, by Daniel Orlick

19020391R00116

Printed in Great Britain
by Amazon